THE NEEDLEWORKER'S COLLECTION

QUICK QUILTS

24 original quilts to make in less than a week

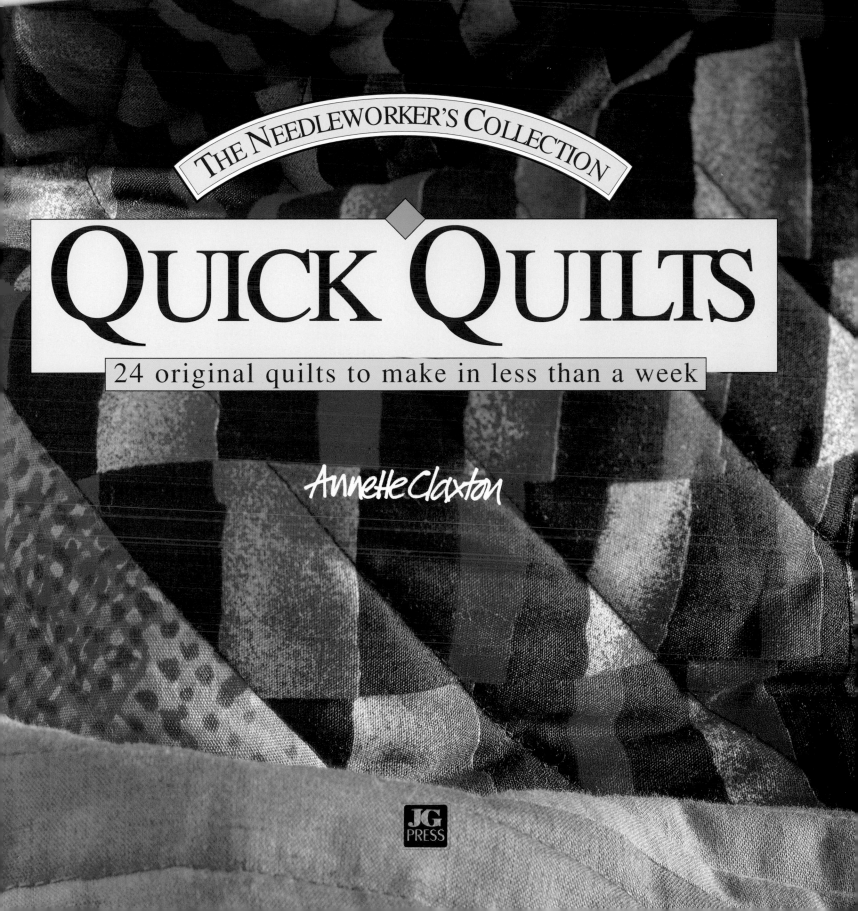

The Needleworker's Collection

QUICK QUILTS

24 original quilts to make in less than a week

Annette Claxton

JG PRESS

CLB 4477
Published in the USA by
JG Press
Distributed by World Publications Inc.
The JG Press imprint is a trademark of JG Press, Inc
455 Somerset Avenue
North Dighton, MA 02764

© 1996 CLB Publishing Godalming, Surrey, England

Printed and bound in Singapore by Tien Wah Press

ISBN 1-57215-153-6

The publishers and author would like to thank Liberty of London Ltd,
Regent Street, London, W1R 6AH for supplying the fabrics on
pages 21-23 (mauve fabric), 61-63, 71-73.

Contents

Introduction

Traditional patchwork and quiltmaking are fascinating but very labour intensive crafts. In this book, however, we have taken into account the demands of modern life and made quiltmaking accessible to everyone who loves to work with textiles. Unique to this book, we have even introduced ways of creating fabric for quilts that are usually applied to other crafts, such as stencilling, dyeing, silk painting, even roller painting.

Always read through the project instructions first, following either metric or imperial measurements – never mix the two as the quilts are slightly different sizes. It is important to wash all the fabrics to avoid shrinkage or colour runs and remove the centre crease. Cut off the selvedge edges, which are more tightly woven and so shrink up, and press well.

Be accurate and consistent in making up your quilt. Stop and correct errors rather than continuing, as mistakes tend to enlarge as the quilt grows.

STARTING OFF

Many of the terms and conventions of quiltmaking will be unfamiliar to beginners and the information below should be read carefully as it is vital to the successful completion of your quilt.

Appliqué is the technique used for applying decorative motifs, usually figurative but sometimes abstract shapes, to a main fabric. These shapes can be applied either by hand or machine or, for speed, by using bonding web, and can be attached to the front or the back of the fabric.

Binding finishes the edges of the quilt with a narrow strip of fabric which can be cut on the straight or bias grain. It can be made from the same fabric as the border or from one of the fabrics used within the body of the quilt. It can also be pieced from many fabrics and used as a final exclamation mark.

Block A block is a unit (usually square) consisting of geometric shapes or figurative designs such as a basket of flowers. Blocks are generally 30cm (12in) square, but can be larger or smaller and are joined together either with or without sashing to make the main quilt. When the blocks are joined edge to edge, new and surprising secondary patterns appear. Blocks can also be joined diagonally, known as "on point".

Borders frame the body of the quilt and can consist of several different widths and fabrics. There are two ways in which borders are attached to the main quilt, squared or butted corners and mitred corners. We give detailed instructions on pages 102–103 for both methods. The area that falls around the mattress is known as "the drop". Borders also serve the useful function of easily enlarging a quilt. Care must be taken, however, not to add extra measurements to the sides without checking that when extra borders are added to the length, the quilt does not become overlong. It is sometimes better to make another line of blocks to widen the quilt.

Cutting plans The cutting plans given in this book are to help readers make the most economical use of their fabric. It is all too easy to start cutting and forget that enough fabric should be left for the borders.

Keep a pair of scissors specially for cutting out fabric – do not use them on paper as this will quickly blunt them. Old rotary blades can be used for paper projects.

Grain refers to the way a fabric has been woven. The weft runs horizontally (right to left), the warp runs from top to bottom. Sometimes the fabric becomes distorted and the pattern is not printed straight so that adjustments have to be made. However, always try to keep the grain of the weave straight, top to bottom or side to side. Try also to cut templates so that the edge that will form the sides of the quilt top is on the straight grain.

Bias grain is the diagonal line running from corner to corner. This part of the weave stretches easily, so is ideal for joining curved seams. On the side of a quilt, however, it will give a very distorted measurement.

Measurements Giving measurements, and a cutting plan where appropriate, at the beginning of the project gives the opportunity of checking that there is enough fabric. If patterned fabrics are being used, take a little time to examine them to establish the repeat and check to see if there is a one way design. Follow the advice "measure twice, cut once!".

Patchwork In patchwork, small, often geometric, units of fabric are joined together to make blocks, which in turn are sewn into a larger whole. Some of the patterns can be traced back many centuries and are seen in tiling, floors, and paintings. Patchwork blocks have been used for well over a hundred years.

Pressing is different from ironing and is an important part of successful patchwork and quiltmaking. Set up an ironing board and steam iron close to the sewing machine and press between every step – do not be tempted to omit or cut down on pressing as the finished quilt will not be nearly as successful without it. Techniques for pressing are given on pages 100–101.

Quilt A quilt consists of two layers of fabric with a thicker layer (known as wadding) between. The top layer may be made from pieces of fabric sewn together into a patchwork or a single piece of material. The wadding can be made from a thin fabric or thick, bonded material. The backing is usually one piece of fabric, but can also be joined to make it large enough, or even pieced to make a patchwork design.

Quilting denotes the stitches that hold the three layers of the quilt together (top, wadding and backing), forming texture and pattern. Hand quilting shows as a line of dots or dashes, whilst machine quilting is an unbroken line. Hand quilting takes longer, but machine quilting is a skill worth acquiring if you like to make speedy quilts.

Sashings Sashings are the pieces of fabric which border blocks, making a frame around each one. They can be cut to any width, a handy way to enlarge a quilt, but are usually within 8cm (3in). Sashings can either be made from a contrasting fabric, or pick up a fabric in the colour or pattern already used in a block.

Seam Allowances All patchwork templates must be cut out to include a seam allowance of at least 7.5mm ($^1/_4$in) extra on all sides. When working with silk, it is advisable to make the allowance a little wider, as the fabric will fray and the seam allowances will get smaller. If the design requires the fabric to be cut out using a template, sew on the pencil line. If fabric is cut out using measurements with the seam allowances included, the edge of the machine foot is used as a guide to measure 7.5mm ($^1/_4$in). Some machines have a useful, special imperial measurement patchwork foot.

Before you begin, be sure to check that the edge of the foot and the precise spot where the needle enters the fabric correspond to the seam allowance measurement specified. Seam allowances are included in rotary cutting calculations unless otherwise stated.

Templates are used as a guide to cutting out the subdivisions of a block or an appliqué motif. The template pattern is transferred onto card or plastic and then onto the fabric, which is then cut out (see page 97).

Wholecloth quilts generally originate from Wales and the North of England. Both areas have traditional designs, sometimes handed down from mother to daughter. Using one cloth, these quilts are hand stitched in intricate patterns and have a quiet beauty of their own.

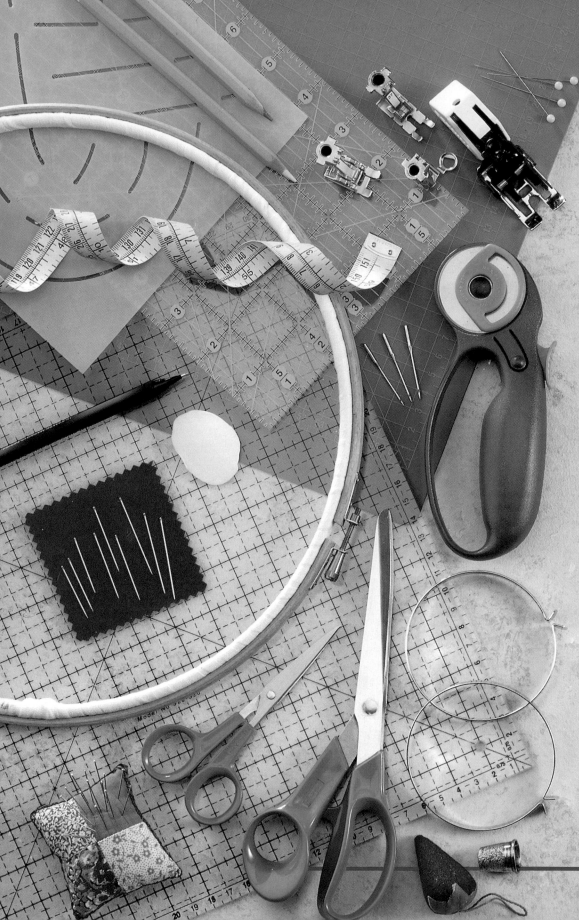

MATERIALS AND EQUIPMENT

Fabrics Fabric should always be pre-washed and pressed before starting to make your quilt. Most fabrics are around 114cm (45in) wide, but sometimes it is more helpful to buy fat quarters for small projects. These measure approximately 57 x 50cm (22 x 18in). Try to get 100 per cent cotton fabric unless otherwise specified to help you to get fuss free results. Cotton is easy to handle, presses beautifully to give crisp seams, and washes and wears well. Dressmaking weight cotton can be used, or even light curtain furnishing fabric.

Backing fabric If possible always use 100 per cent cotton fabric to back a quilt. Sheeting is available in wide widths, but is not such a good idea as it is very densely woven and not easy to sew, either by hand or machine. Using a wide backing is, however, a great time saver. Good quality cotton 228cm (90in) wide would require just the length for a double quilt, 152cm (60in) wide for a single. However, horizontal or vertical joins with the selvedge removed can be made from the narrower widths (see page 103). Always wash the backing as well as the top fabrics to allow for shrinkage and to test for dye fastness.

Wadding or batting is hidden inside a quilt and gives a quilt its loft (or springiness). Always buy a good quality wadding, as some of the cheaper versions will migrate through to the outside, spoiling hours of work. Wadding comes in different weights, from 60–220g (2–8oz), and in widths from 90–152cm (36–60in). It is quicker to buy the wadding the size of your bed quilt (single, queen or king size) as the narrow widths require joining. Dark-coloured wadding should be used when working on dark fabrics to minimize the effect of fibres working through and showing on the front. Always allow at least 5cm (2in) more wadding on all sides of the quilt to allow for shrinkage. Needlepoint and cotton domette are types of wadding.

Polyfelt hangs well in clothing, needle punch is suitable for wallhangings, silk is light, and both cotton and wool are available in various weights with or without the addition of polyester. Domette, an interfacing used in tailoring is also used as a wadding. It comes as both a flat (woven), and a fluffy, knitted version. The amount of "puff" seen on a quilt after it has been quilted is known as loft, so the flatter the wadding, the lower the loft.

Rotary cutters, self-healing cutting mats and acrylic rulers have revolutionized strip piecing. The rotary cutter can be used freehand with or without a guide. Do cultivate a good working practice and always close the safety guard after each cut as the blade is very sharp and could cause a nasty accident. Seam allowances are usually included in rotary cutting calculations.

The rulers, which are printed with accurate vertical and horizontal lines as well as 30 and 60 degree angles, come in many lengths and widths in both imperial and metric measurements. Smaller versions of all three are made for quilters who like to take their work wherever they go. There are also several sizes of square rules with lines to help with cutting squares and log cabin piecing, together with a diagonal centre line for cutting triangles and bias. The large square rule helps with cutting straight edges on finished blocks. A variety of other rules help with making triangles and other designs based on strip piecing.

Pins Most of the projects are constructed by machining over pins. Buy fine dressmaking pins for sewing and fine glasshead pins for pintacking the quilt. Safety pins can be used but be careful that they do not leave large holes which will weaken the fabric. Buy the finest quality you can find.

Needles Change the needle in your machine frequently and always at the start of a new project, as pins from a previous project will have blunted the point. Keep a stock of good quality size 80 (12) and 90 (14) needles in your workbox and expect to use between three to four needles per quilt. Size 80 (12) can be used for most threads, but for thicker or buttonhole threads use size 90 (14). Buying needles by the box is economical in both time and money.

Threads Use a 50 mercerized cotton thread for both piecing and quilting in most of the projects. Grey can be used for medium tone colours, light or medium cream for light colours, and sometimes it is better to match your thread with brightly coloured fabric. Grey and cream can be bought on economical 1,000m (1,000yd) reels. Buttonhole, embroidery and machine threads are specified for some projects. For quilts where a coloured thread would be intrusive, use fine nylon monofilament, with cotton thread on the bobbin. Hand quilting requires a strong thread specially made either in cotton or cotton covered polyester.

Sewing machine One of the ways in which we have been able to make the quilts in this book so quickly is by machine piecing and quilting. This can be done on a domestic model, but without doubt a larger motor is a great help. The sewing machine is your best friend, your right hand, so take time to get to know it well.

A walking foot, although expensive, makes machine quilting very much easier. To understand its function, examine the serrated "feed dogs" below the sewing machine needle. Each time the machine makes a stitch, the feed dogs move the fabric backwards. At the point when the feed dogs drop and let go of the material, the walking foot presses down and gently holds it in place, stopping it from puckering or slipping. The walking foot also has a useful guide for parallel lines.

Free machine quilting, such as is used for the Cherub Quilt on page 78, dispenses with the feed dogs altogether. Techniques for machine quilting are given on page 106.

Miscellaneous In addition to sewing materials, you will also need equipment for making templates, including 5cm (2in) dressmaker's graphpaper, card, template plastic, and sharp pencils and a waterproof pen. For marking quilting lines, use either a quilter's marker pencil, or save slivers of soap, as these make good markers, whose lines can then be washed off.

THE FINISHED QUILT

Labels should be sewn onto the back of your quilt, with your name, date and the quilt's name. Labels can be handwritten using laundry pens, embroidered by hand or machine, pieced, painted or photocopied and printed.

Hanging quilts on walls needs a little thought. If the quilt is in direct sunlight, it will fade very quickly. However this can sometimes give a charming effect. The easiest way to hang a quilt is by attaching a sleeve along the top of the quilt back (see page 107) and sliding a flat batten through it. The batten should be cut just short of the sides of the quilt and can rest on two picture hook pins.

Storage Quilts should never be stored in plastic bags as they tend to rot in time. Cover carpet inner tubes with offcuts of wadding, then wrap the quilt around with the right side to the outside and finish with an old cotton sheet.

Cleaning Wall quilts can be vacuumed regularly, using the upholstery attachment, but covering the nozzle with old stocking or tights. Silk quilts should be dry cleaned, but be sure to impress on the cleaners that they must not be pressed, or the quilt will be flattened. Wadding manufacturers do not advise dry cleaning for cot quilts in case cleaning fluid fumes are retained.

Two pairs of hands are needed to wash a quilt as the wet quilts are very heavy, which puts considerable strain on the quilting stitches. On a warm day fill a bath with cool water, then add a gentle soap powder. Loosely fold the quilt and place it in the bath. Gently squeeze the quilt with the flat of your hands. Drain the dirty water and refill with rinsing water. Continue in this way until the water seems clean. Carefully lift the quilt into an old baby bath or large plastic bag and carry it outside. Fix up a couple of parallel lines and drape the quilt over until the main water has drained out. Reposition the quilt and shake from time to time so that the clothes lines do not make marks. Do not leave the quilt in strong sunlight as the colours will fade. Do not iron as the creases will gradually disappear.

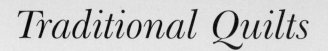

Traditional Quilts

Strong graphic lines are a feature of traditional quilts. Here are five which offer the opportunity for new and experienced quilters to achieve exciting, fast results.

Twisting Amish Fans

Amish quilts are admired throughout the world for their original use of colour and we have taken one of these combinations to use as a lively wallhanging. The curves are quick and simple to piece and the machine quilting which uses two different thread colours, is not difficult. The finished size of this quilt is 134cm (54in) square, but by adding more blocks and a wider border, it could be made into a bed quilt. Seam allowances of 7.5mm (¹/₄in) will need to be added to the templates.

WORKBASKET

❖

6 fat quarters (57 x 50cm/22 x 18in) cotton fabric, 3 in yellow, orange and tan, 3 in darker shades of ginger, rust and tan

❖

2.4m (2³/₄yd) rich blue cotton fabric 114cm (45in) wide

❖

25cm (¹/₄yd) red cotton fabric 114cm wide (45in) wide

❖

1.5m (1³/₄yd) cotton backing fabric 150cm (60in) wide

❖

150cm (60in) square needlepunch wadding

❖

1 reel grey cotton thread for piecing

❖

1 reel each of blue and orange cotton thread for machine quilting

❖

Template plastic 30cm (12in) square

❖

Double-sided sticky tape

❖

Dressmaker's 5cm (2in) graphpaper

❖

Waterproof pen

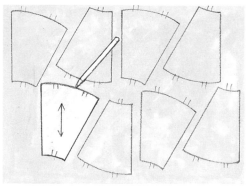

1 *Following the instructions on page 97, enlarge the fan block on page 19 to 30cm (12in) square on dressmaker's graphpaper, and trace it onto template plastic using a waterproof pen. Number the pieces and draw in balance marks (the tiny double marks) and grain lines. Cut out on the drawn line and attach a piece of double-sided sticky tape to the back of each template. Do not leave the sticky tape on the fabric overnight as it will stain.*

One at a time, place template numbers 1, 2 and 3 on the wrong side of the yellow, orange and tan fabrics, and on the ginger, rust and tan fabrics, ensuring the straight edge is on the grain. On each colour draw around the template eight times, using a sharp pencil and leaving a seam allowance of 7.5mm (¹/₄in) around each piece. Repeat for template numbers 4 and 5 on the rich blue fabric.

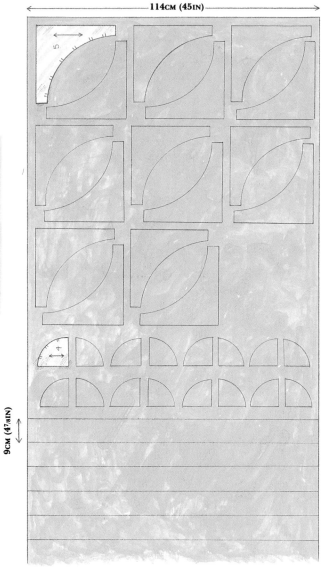

2 *Following the cutting plan for the main (blue) fabric, place the large template (no.5) as shown. Draw around the template 16 times, using a sharp white pencil, leaving a seam allowance of approximately 7.5mm (¹/₄in) between each one. Next draw around the small, curved corner template (no.4) 16 times as above. Cut out all the pieces and sort them into separate piles.*

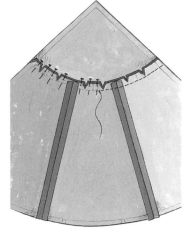

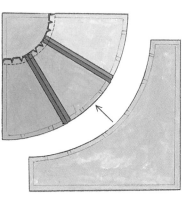

3 *Join the fan shapes together in the order shown. Prepare to chain stitch (see page 100) by pinning all the shapes, and machine stitching together. Press (see page 100).*

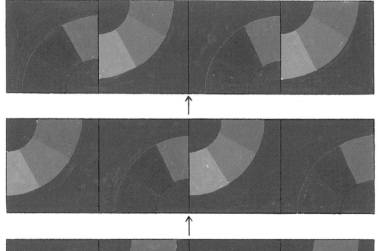

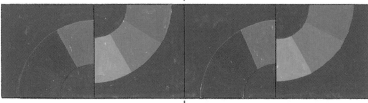

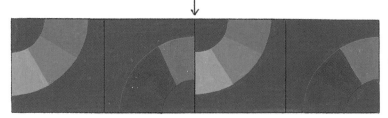

4 *When sewing curves, it is necessary to sew on the lines drawn around the templates. Join the pieced fans to the curved corner pieces. The top fabric will need to stretch around the curve, so snip into the seam allowance, being very careful not to cut as far as the seam line. Pin well, being sure to have the sides and balance marks correctly aligned, and check that the drawn lines on each piece match. Use plenty of pins as shown in the diagram and machine sew over them. Check for accuracy, correct, then press. Continue chain sewing until 16 are finished.*

5 *Lastly, add the final blue piece, template 5, matching the balance marks. Pin and machine stitch. Press well and check the squares are the right size.*

6 *Join the blocks together in rows of four, press, then join the rows together to make a 121.5cm (48¹/₂in) square. Press well.*

From the red fabric cut five strips 4cm (1¹/₂in) wide and join to make two red borders 121.5 x 4cm (48¹/₂ x 1¹/₂in) and two 127 x 4cm (50¹/₂ x 1¹/₂in). Pin and sew the shorter pair to the top and bottom and the longer pair to the two sides as shown on pages 102–103. Press.

Cut five border lengths, as it will be necessary to join them up, then cut four borders, two 126.5 x 9cm (50¹/₂ x 3¹/₂in) long and two 141.5 x 9cm (56¹/₂ x 3¹/₂in) long. Add the four borders (see pages 102–103). Give the pieced top its final press.

7 *Trace the quilting guide, which is shown by dotted lines on the template, onto template plastic. Cut out on the lines and put some double-sided sticky tape on the back of each piece. Place the templates on the quilt top and mark the quilting lines, using a sliver of soap. The curves should flow from the edge of the piecing, across the plain areas.*

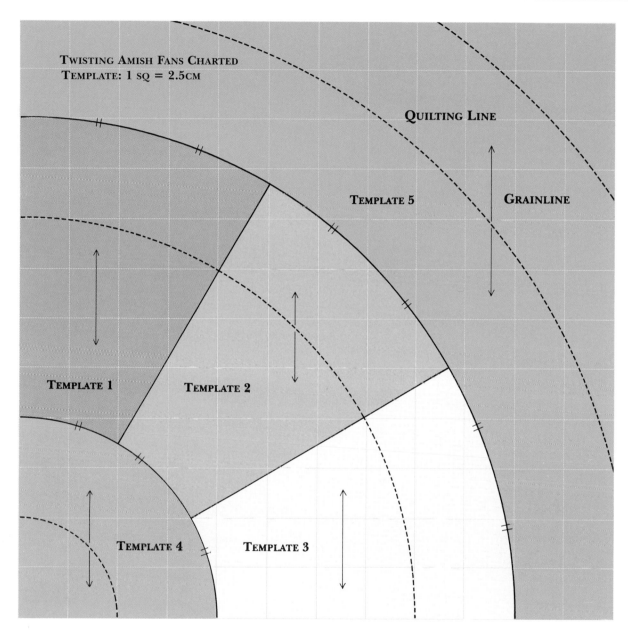

TWISTING AMISH FANS CHARTED
TEMPLATE: 1 SQ = 2.5CM

QUILTING LINE

TEMPLATE 5

GRAINLINE

TEMPLATE 1

TEMPLATE 2

TEMPLATE 4

TEMPLATE 3

Follow the directions for sandwiching and pintacking the three layers of the quilt on page 104. Using a neutral thread on the bobbin, machine quilt (see page 106), using orange thread close to and on the fans. Pull the ends of the threads through to the back and tie (see page 106). Change to blue thread and quilt the areas between, following the guide lines and allowing the lines to flow off the edge of the fabric. These threads will not need tying. After quilting, straighten the edges of the wadding and backing (see page 102), trim, turn a seam allowance to the back and slip stitch. Finally sew on a hanging sleeve (see page 107).

Log Cabin

Pretty fabrics in soft appealing colours give a gentle effect in this ingenious log cabin quilt. The "logs" are worked around a sprigged floral motif over wadding, so that the quilting is sewn in one step, a time-saving technique known as Quilt-As-You-Go. If pressed with an iron the wadding would flatten, so finger pressing is used instead. Use a patterned fabric for the backing so that the machined lines will blend into the background. The blocks are arranged in the traditional set, known as "Straight Furrows". The finished size of the quilt is 217 x 155cm (84 x 60 in). The quilt could be made into a double size by making more blocks.

The Log Cabin is one of the most traditional and most recognized of quilt blocks, treasured for the variety of patterns that can be created, and for the wonderful texture of the quilted logs. This simple method of piecing the quilt not only means that assembly is easy, but also that quilting and piecing are done at the same time!

WORKBASKET
❖

50cm (¹/2yd) sprig-flowered cotton fabric 114cm (45in) wide
❖
3m (3¹/2yd) yellow flowered cotton fabric 114cm (45in) wide
❖
3m (3¹/2yd) lilac flowered cotton fabric 114cm (45in) wide
❖
4m (4¹/2yd) patterned cotton backing fabric 114cm (45in) wide
❖
6.7m (7¹/2yd) light wadding 90cm (39in) wide
❖
4 reels white cotton thread
❖
Card
❖
B Pencil

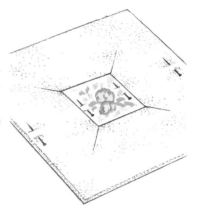

1 *Cut out 35 33cm (13in) squares from the backing fabric and wadding, using the rotary cutter, quilter's rule and cutting mat for speed (see page 99). Make a window template 9cm (3¹/2in) square from card to use for the middle of the block. Cut out a centre square through which the motifs can be framed. Place on the right side of the floral sprigged fabric, so that a floral motif is placed centrally in the window. Draw around the outside of the template, using a fine pencil. Repeat and cut out 35 such centre squares. Using the rotary cutter and rule (see page 99) cut out 5cm (2in) wide strips from both the yellow and lilac flowered fabrics. Use all the fabric, cutting from selvedge edge to edge. Organize your materials so that you can work efficiently and quickly. Hang the strips on coathangers and use up the short lengths, saving the longer pieces for the edges of the block.*

2 *Place the wadding over the backing square and, using a B pencil, draw a diagonal cross in the centre, measuring from corner to corner.*

3 *Centre the floral sprig square on the wadding and backing so that each corner touches a drawn line. Pin in place.*

4 *Take a yellow strip and place right sides together across the top of the centre square. Pin then sew as far as the end of the square, making a double stitch to start and finish. A double stitch is made using a reverse stitch. Fold back the excess strip to align with the edge of the square and finger press to make a line. Trim the strip level with the side of the square. Take out the pins and finger press (see page 100) the strip upwards. Turn the work a quarter turn anticlockwise.*

Log Cabin

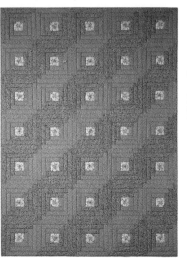

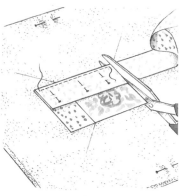

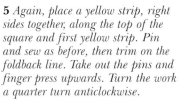

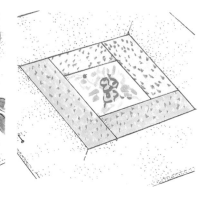

5 *Again, place a yellow strip, right sides together, along the top of the square and first yellow strip. Pin and sew as before, then trim on the foldback line. Take out the pins and finger press upwards. Turn the work a quarter turn anticlockwise.*

6 *Now take a lilac strip and pin right sides together along the top of the square and second yellow strip. Sew as before. Trim, fold upwards and finger press. Turn the work a quarter turn anticlockwise.*

7 *Work the final side of the square, which now includes a lilac and two yellow strips, in the same way as shown above, completing one round of the log cabin block.*

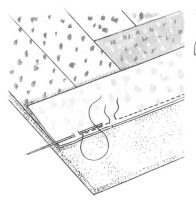

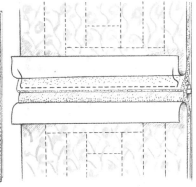

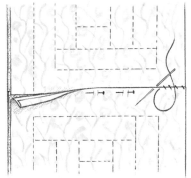

8 *Work two more rounds of logs, always attaching the yellow strips on the opposite side to the lilac strips. On the final round stop sewing 2.5cm (1in) from the end of the last strip. These ends must be detached from the wadding for the quilt-as-you-go method of joining the blocks. When the logs on all 35 blocks have been sewn, work a few hand or machine stitches to finish the ends of the strips on each square.*

9 *Lay out all the blocks in seven rows of five blocks, so that a secondary design of diagonal lines appears. This is known as "Straight Furrows". Keeping the blocks in order, place the blocks in pairs, right sides together. Pin back the wadding and backing, then pin and sew the pieced blocks together, matching seam lines accurately.*

10 *Open out the two blocks and finger press the seam line. Trim the wadding, so that there is a slight overlap between the two blocks. Sew a running stitch to join the two, without catching the lower fabric.*

11 *Working from the back, fold in a seam allowance, centring over the seam on the front by pushing a pin through as a guide. Slip stitch, sewing through the wadding, but not to the front fabric.*

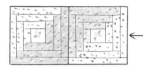 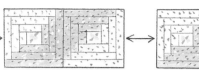 

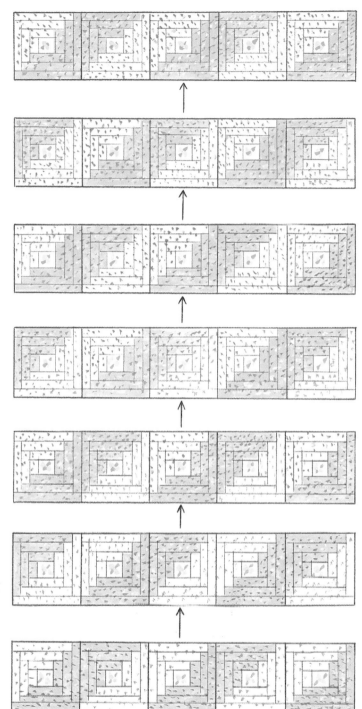

12 *Join the pairs together in a strip and join the remaining single block to the end of the strip in the same way as before.*

13 *Finally, join the strips together. Neatly trim the edges of the quilt (see page 102).*

14 *Measure the sides and top and bottom of the quilt and cut binding strips 4cm (1¹/₄in) wide, joining them if necessary. Press in a 7.5mm (¹/₄in) seam allowance on one side of the strips (see page 102 "Folding towards the back"). Sew the binding strip to the edge of the quilt, right sides together, then fold to the back and pin. Machine or hand sew.*

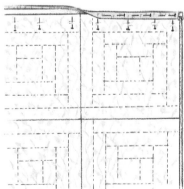

Blues in the Night

The nine-patch block shown here is made from space-dyed fabric in colours ranging from blue through mauve to green and turquoise and is alternated with a co-ordinating geometric single fabric square. The fabric used here was purchased, but it would be possible for you to space dye your own fabric as described on page 42. It is a great way to add excitement to this simple block. The finished quilt measures 245 x 202cm (97 x 80in).

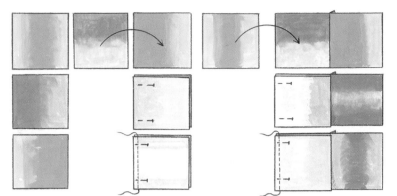

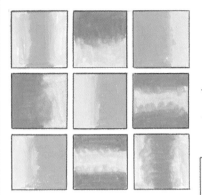

1 *Wash the fabrics and press. Using the rotary cutting method, described on page 99, cut 20 11.5cm (4¹/₂in) wide strips from the space-dyed fabric. Cut the strips into 180 11.5cm (4¹/₂in) squares (see page 99). Arrange them in 20 blocks of nine squares each, distributing the colours evenly.*

WORKBASKET
❖

2.4m (2²/₃yd) blue/turquoise space-dyed cotton fabric 114cm (45in) wide
❖
2.4m (2²/₃yd) geometric-patterned co-ordinating cotton fabric 114cm (45in) wide
❖
2.2m (2¹/₂yd) striped cotton border fabric 114cm (45in) wide
❖
4.8m (5¹/₃yd) cotton backing fabric 60in wide
❖
245 x 202cm (97 x 80in) wadding
❖
2 reels grey cotton thread for piecing
❖
2 reels dark blue cotton thread for machine quilting

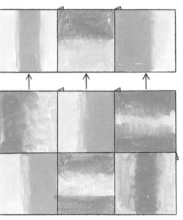

4 *Join the bottom and middle strips together and finally join the top row together. Press well.*

Following the instructions on page 99, cut four strips 31.5cm (12¹/₂in) wide from the geometric patterned fabric. Cut into 12 31.5cm (12¹/₂in) squares (A). Cut three strips 32.5cm (12⁷/₈in) wide and cut into seven squares (B). Cut one 33.5cm (13¹/₄in) square (C). Cut diagonally across the seven larger squares (B) to make 14 triangles (see page 99). Next cut twice diagonally across the single square (C), making four quarter triangles for the quilt corners.

2 *For each block, place all the centre squares, wrong side up, over the right hand squares and hold with two horizontal pins. Chain piece as shown on page 100. Check each one for accuracy, correct if necessary (it is always easier to make corrections as you go along) and press the seams to one side (see page 100). Lay all the squares out again in blocks of nine.*

3 *Place the left-hand squares over the centre squares, pin and then chain piece and, following the routine check, press.*

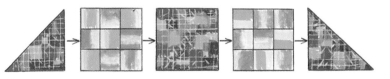

5 *Join the pieced and patterned squares together in 8 strips, referring to the diagram in step 7 to establish how many squares in each row. Following the diagram, add a triangle (B) at each end.*

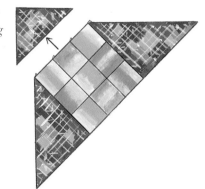

6 *Finally join the small triangles (C) to form the corners of the quilt. Two of the triangles are joined to the top of each single block strip and the remaining two are joined at opposite ends of the two central strips.*

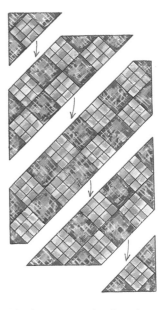

7 *Join the rows together in pairs, matching the joins. Press well.*

From the striped border fabric cut two borders 214.5 x 20cm (85½ x 8in) and two 212 x 20cm (84½ x 8in). Attach to the quilt as shown on pages 102–103.

Press well before marking up with diagonal quilting lines across the patterned squares. Extend the diagonal quilting design into the borders by 15cm (6in). Sandwich the top, wadding and backing together and pin tack (see page 104).

Using the walking foot and dark blue thread, quilt (see page 106) continuously up and down the quilting lines and border seams, starting from the centre line and pivoting at corners (see page 107). Machine quilt in the ditch (see page 106) along the border seams.

Square off the quilt 15cm (6in) from the border quilting line to the edge. Trim. Turn the border fabric to the back, slip stitch.

Star Quilt

The arrangement and colours chosen for this wonderfully eccentric star block have their roots in Afro-American quilts. These quilts were made from any available bits of fabric and have a special charm of their own. We have used checked Indian cotton in two colourways, together with black fabric, which makes the colours sing. You will see that two of the stars are made up in black and one block has the star points reversed. The width of the sashing varies and two blocks are joined together without any at all! The finished wallhanging measures 160cm (63in) square.

WORKBASKET

❖

2.1m (2¹/₃yd) pink checked Indian cotton fabric 114cm (45in) wide

❖

70cm (³/₄yd) pink/turquoise checked Indian cotton 114cm (45in) wide

❖

50cm (¹/₂yd) blue/green checked Indian cotton fabric 114cm (45in) wide

❖

2m (2yd) black cotton fabric 114cm (45in) wide

❖

3.3m (3¹/₂yd) cotton backing fabric 114cm (45in) wide, joined to make a 125cm (65in) square

❖

4m (4yd) needlepunch wadding 90cm (36in) wide, joined to make a 125cm (65in) square

❖

2 reels grey cotton thread

Use the quick rotary cutting method (see page 99) to cut out border strips, squares and triangles as described below. From the pink checked fabric, cut strips 10cm (3⁷/₈in) wide and divide into 33 squares. Stack four or five squares on top of each other and cut diagonally into 66 triangles (see page 99) for piece A (Star Block on page 29). Cut strips 16.5cm (6¹/₂in) wide to make eight squares (piece B). Cut two 18.5cm (7¹/₄in) squares and divide into four triangles (piece D). Cut four 9cm (3¹/₂in) squares (piece C).

From the blue checked fabric, cut strips 10cm (3⁷/₈in) wide to make 23 squares, then cut diagonally as before to make 46 triangles (piece A). Cut six 16.5cm (6¹/₂in) squares (piece B), four 9cm (3¹/₂in) squares (piece C) and two 18.5cm (7¹/₄in) squares. Divide these last into four triangles (piece D). From the black fabric, cut strips 10cm (3⁷/₈in) wide to make eight squares. Cut diagonally to make 17 triangles (piece A). Cut strips 9cm (3¹/₂in) wide to make 56 squares (piece C). Cut strips 18.5cm (7¹/₄in) wide to make 56 triangles (piece D). Cut two 16.5cm (6¹/₂in) squares.

2 *Now join a black square C to either side of half of the pieced triangles, adding the coloured squares to either side of the "rogue" star pieces.*

1 *Using the chain piecing method (see page 100), join a coloured piece A to one short side of each black D piece as shown. Snip apart the chain and press seams towards piece A. Join another pink or turquoise piece A to the other short side of each black D piece.*

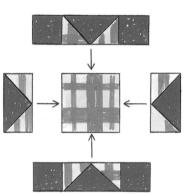

3 *Join the remaining pieced triangles to the top and bottom of matching square Bs. This can again be done chain fashion. Join the three strips together to finish each star block. Watch out for the reversed points block!*

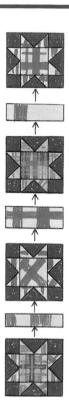

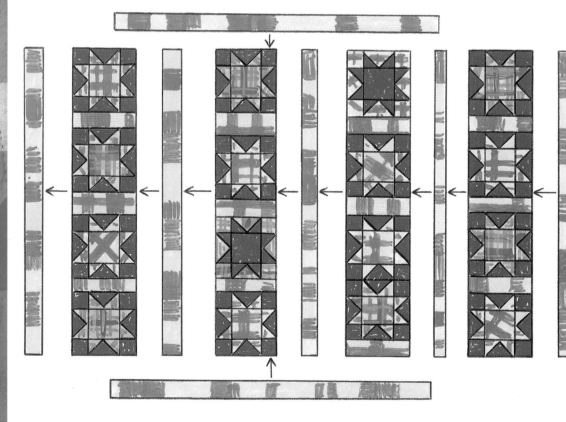

4 *(Above). From the remainder of the pink checked fabric, cut from across the width 12 short sashings 31.5cm (12¹/₂in) long: ten 9cm (3¹/₂in) wide, one 11.5cm (4¹/₂in) wide and one 6.5cm (2¹/₂in) wide. Join together the blocks and sashings in rows from top to bottom.*

5 *(Left). Next, add the sashings to join the strips vertically in the centre and at the sides.*

From the pink checked fabric, cut five borders 144.5cm (57¹/₂in) long: three 9.5cm (3¹/₂in) wide, one 12cm (4¹/₂in) wide and one 15.5cm (2in) wide. Cut two borders 170 x 9.5cm (63¹/₂ x 3¹/₂in). Cut four binding strips 170 x 4cm (64 x 1¹/₂in). Referring to the techniques on pages 102–103, add the borders using the butt corner method.

6 *Mark up for quilting with freehand fan shapes, starting around the edge and filling in the centre. We hand quilted the lines about 2.5cm (1in) apart but diagonal, ditch or grid machine quilting would be fast and just as effective. Layer together the top, wadding and backing as shown on page 102. Finally, square up, trim the edges (see page 104) and bind as shown on pages 103–104.*

The template below may help you to organize the star block pieces for the quilt more easily. It could also be used as a more efficient way of cutting fabric for making a smaller piece of patchwork, such as a cushion cover.

STAR QUILT CHARTED TEMPLATE:
1 SQ = 2.5CM (1IN)

The star block is one of the most popular for sewing a quilt. With quick cutting and machine techniques the quilt is easily made in just a few days, but remember to work methodically and carefully press after each step.

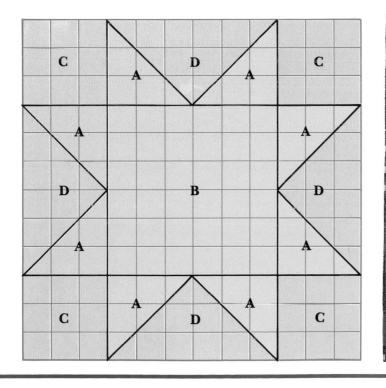

Birds in the Air

This charming traditional block uses a combination of new and scrap pieces of fabric collected together over several years, and donated by friends and relatives. The quilt has been designed in colours that move from dark to light to give the impression of a flock of birds flying towards the sky. A quick method of cutting triangles and a fast piecing system makes time itself fly. The finished quilt measures 223 x 162cm (88 x 76in).

WORKBASKET
✤

30 scrap cotton fabrics in a variety of colours from dark to light at least 30 x 16cm (12 x 6in)

✤

3m (3½yd) dark red cotton fabric 114cm (45in) wide

✤

1.8m (2yd) co-ordinating light cotton fabric 114cm (45in) wide

✤

4.8m (5⅓yd) cotton backing fabric 114cm (45in) wide

✤

275 x 230cm (108 x 90in) wadding

✤

2 reels grey cotton thread for piecing

✤

2 reels dark red cotton thread for machine quilting

✤

Card

✤

Spray adhesive

✤

Dressmaker's 5cm (2in) graphpaper

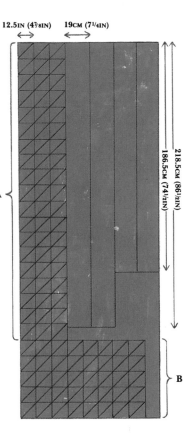

12.5IN (4⅞IN)   19CM (7¼IN)

218.5CM (86½IN)

186.5CM (73½IN)

A

B

A 18 ROWS OF 3
SQUARES = 108 TRIANGLES
B 5 ROWS OF 8
SQUARES = 80 TRIANGLES

1 *The red triangles are speedily cut using the rotary cutter. Following the cutting diagram, first cut strips 12.5cm (4⅞in) wide from the red fabric and divide into 90 squares (see page 99). Then divide these diagonally (see page 99) to make 180 triangles. On completion of the quilt top, four borders will be cut from the red cotton fabric. The large contrast triangles are cut in a similar manner from the co-ordinating light fabric. Cut strips 32.5cm (12⅞in) wide and divide them into 15 32.5cm (12⅞in) squares. Cut diagonally across each square to make 30 triangles (see page 99).*

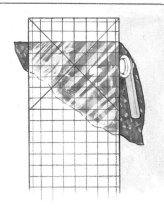

2 *Place the ruler on one of the scraps of fabric and, using the rotary cutter and board, cut two right angle sides on the straight grain of the fabric.*

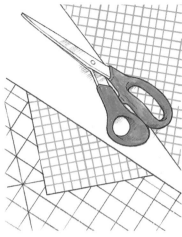

3 *To make the small triangle template, measure on graphpaper 12.5cm (4⁷/8in) at right angles and then join the two points with a diagonal line. This measurement will include a seam allowance of 7.5mm (¹/4in) seam allowance on all sides. Cut out and stick to a cutting ruler or bias square with spray adhesive.*

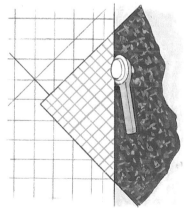

4 *Place the right angles of the template over those of the scrap. Cut along the long diagonal side of the triangle. Repeat steps 2 and 4 to cut three triangles from each scrap, being sure to keep the grainline straight. Continue until there are three triangles from each of the 30 scrap fabrics.*

Birds in the Air

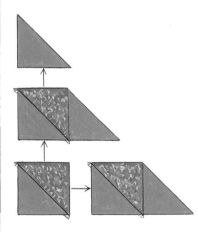

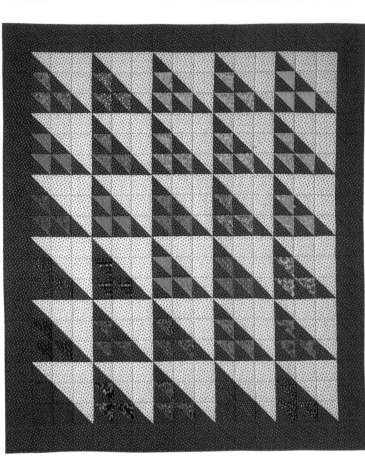

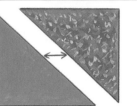

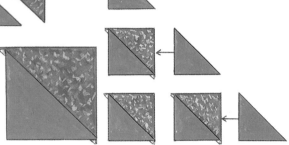

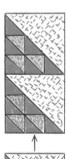

5 *Pin, right sides together, all the scrap triangles to a red triangle on the diagonal (long) side and piece chain fashion (see page 100). Check for accuracy and press the seam allowance towards the main colour fabric (see page 100).*

6 *Working methodically, lay out the elements of the pieced triangle in each block, with three scrap "birds" in each. Pin a small red triangle to the right hand side of two of the squares in each block. Sew all these chain method.*

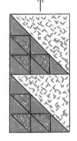

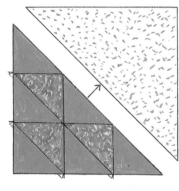

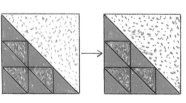

7 *Add the final pieced square to the corner, then join the three units to make the large pieced triangle.*

8 *Join the pieced triangle to the large contrast triangle with a diagonal seam. Press the seams open. The finished square should measure 31.5cm (12½in).*

9 *Lay out all the blocks and arrange them to give a diagonal gradation from light fabric to dark fabric. Join in pairs.*

10 *Working one strip at a time, join two pairs and a single block to make each strip of blocks.*

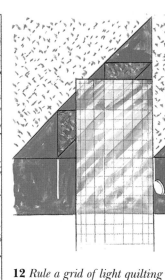

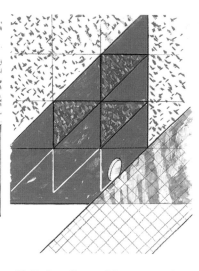

12 *Rule a grid of light quilting guidelines with a sharp quilter's pencil across the large light coloured triangles. Use the seam lines as guides on the pieced areas. Use a small sliver of soap to mark the sawtooth detail on the darker border, extending the grid onto the border by 10cm (4in).*

13 *Rule a diagonal line to join the grid quilting lines marked on the border, including one between the grid lines at each corner.*

11 *Pin, then sew these strips of five blocks together.*

Measure the sides of the quilt and, compensating for any discrepancy (see page 102), cut borders from the red fabric 19cm (7½in) wide, two 218.5cm (86½in) and two 186.5cm (74½in) long. Attach mitred borders (see page 103).

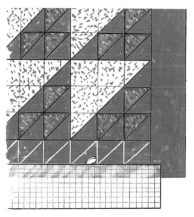

14 *Mark a line around the edge of the border, connecting the marked grid lines. Prepare for quilting following the layering instructions on page 104.*

It will be easier to quilt Birds in the Air in two steps. Using the walking foot, first quilt the straight line grid,

starting with a centre line. Sew a few tiny stitches, then lengthen the stitch and continue to the end, finishing with a few tiny stitches.

When the grid is complete, work the sawtooth border. Starting from one corner with a few tiny stitches, extend one of the straight lines to the point, and leaving the needle in place, pivot the quilt and work the diagonal line back towards the border seam line. Leave the needle in place and pivot again down a straight line, continuing to work alternate diagonal and straight lines until the border is finished.

To finish, trim the top, backing and wadding straight (see page 102), and turn the border fabric to the back. Pin, turning under a 7.5mm (¼in) hem, then machine in place along the edge from the wrong side.

Creating Fabric

It has never been easier to create fabrics with new, user-friendly paints. From stencilled poppies to silk-painted patchwork, these quilts are exciting and unique.

Poppies

The large oriental poppies on this quilt are easily made by spraying with car paints through a stencil. Surprisingly, the car paint does not give a hard finish, and as we have used cotton polyester, the quilt will hand wash and remain uncreased. Before starting, read the instructions carefully, then lightly spray a practice piece on a spare square of fabric. The blocks are individually quilted using the quilt-as-you-go method, which can be worked by hand or machine, with free-machine quilting, or with the walking foot. The finished size of the quilt is 208 x 171cm (82 x 68in), but it can be enlarged on all sides by attaching wider borders.

The seam allowances on this quilt are 12mm (1/2in).

WORKBASKET

❖

4.5m (4¹/₂yd) cotton polyester sheeting 228cm (90in) wide

❖

1m (1yd) green cotton polyester 277cm (109in) wide

❖

6.5m (6¹/₂yd) high loft wadding 90cm (39in) wide

❖

4 reels white, 1 reel pale green polyester thread

❖

Car paint sprays in red, green and black

❖

Dressmaker's 5cm (2in) graphpaper

❖

Black fabric-painting pen

❖

Waterproof pen

❖

Masking tape

❖

Spray adhesive

❖

Template plastic 46cm (18in) square

1 *Enlarge the poppy diagram on page 39 by transferring it onto 5cm (2in) graphpaper as shown on page 97. Cut a piece of template plastic to 46cm (18in) square. Measure and make register marks at the corners 12mm (1/2in) from the edges to make a 42cm (17in) square, under which the fabric square will fit. Place the design on a flat surface and hold in place with masking tape. Centre the template plastic over the design and trace the design onto it, using a waterproof pen. Mark the top of the design with an X.*

2 *Using a sharp craft knife, carefully cut out the stencil flowers, leaves and stalks. Any accidental cuts can be mended with masking tape. Place the stencil on a large sheet of paper and draw round the three black poppy centres. Cut these out to use as a mask when spraying the black centres. Additional masks for the poppies and leaves may also come in useful.*

Using the rotary cutter method (see page 99) cut 40 42cm (17in) squares of white cotton polyester. Cut 20 squares the same size from wadding. Put 20 white squares to one side for the backing fabric.

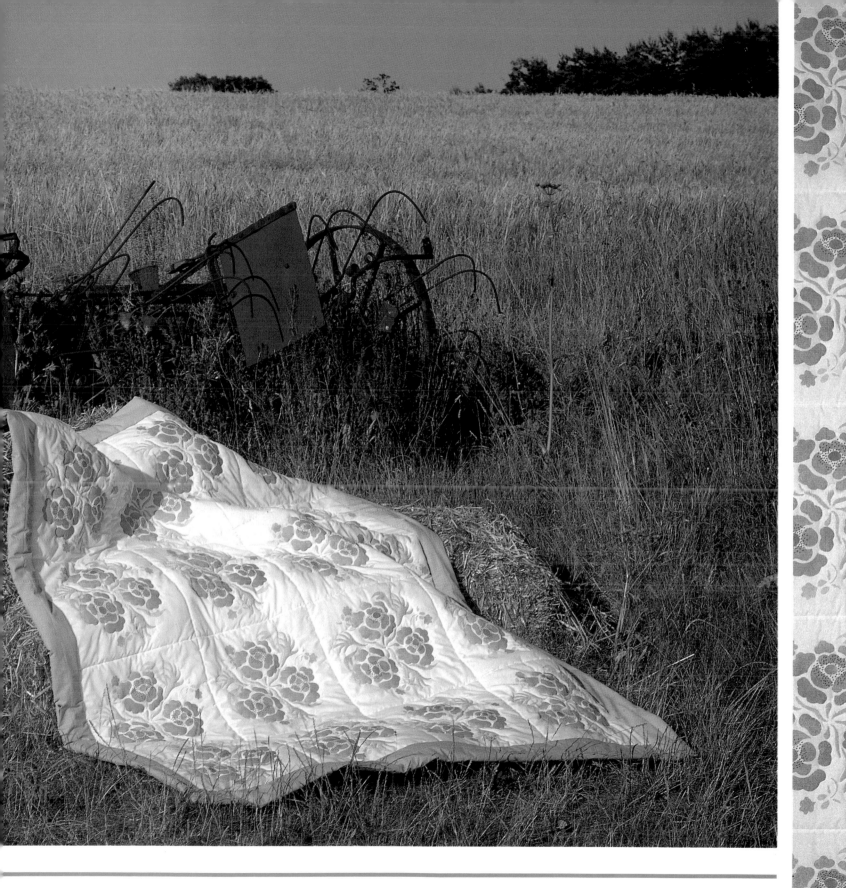

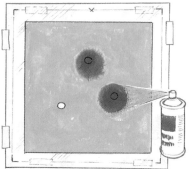

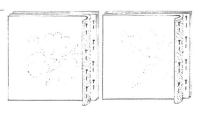

3 *Cover a table with newspaper and spray a thin coat of adhesive onto the back of the stencil. Place the first square of fabric on the table right side up. Using the register marks on the stencil, centre the design sticky side down over the fabric. Cover it with the mask cut in step 2. Shake the spray can of black paint and lightly spray the three poppy centres. Put to one side to dry. Repeat on all 20 squares.*

4 *Next spray the poppies. Register the stencil over the black centres then shake the red spray. Aim the paint at the petals from a distance of about 20cm (8in), holding a piece of folded paper in the other hand to protect the green leaves. Do not worry if the red drifts onto the green leaves. Repeat on all 20 squares and put to one side to dry. Spray the green leaves, using the same technique to protect the poppies from green paint. When all the squares are finished, use the black fabric-painting pen to draw in black dots around the poppy centres.*

5 *Prepare to quilt by sandwiching one wadding square between a backing and poppy square, matching all sides. Pin around the edges, then on the stalks, working out a continuous quilting route around the leaves to avoid tying off too many ends. Free-machine or hand quilt around the edges of the stalks and leaves (see page 106). When these are complete, pin around the flowers in the same way and quilt in a continuous line. Continue sewing until 20 blocks are completed. Pull the end threads through to the back and knot (see page106). The blocks may have distorted slightly, so after quilting trim the edges to 42cm (16in) square (see page 102).*

6 *Mark the top of each block with a couple of pins and lay out in five horizontal strips of four squares each. Keeping the blocks in order, place them in pairs, right sides together. Pin the wadding and backing out of the way, and pin then sew the poppy squares with a 12mm (¹/2in) seam allowance. These can be worked chain fashion (see page 100). Finger press the seams open (see page 100). Lay out the pairs and sew together to make five rows of four blocks.*

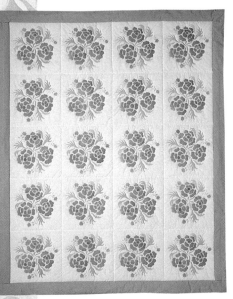

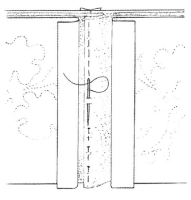

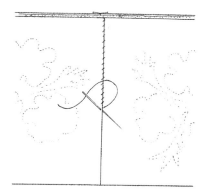

7 *Turn the lengths over, pin the backing fabric out of the way then overlap the wadding between each block, making sure the poppy blocks below are flat. Sew with a medium-sized running stitch (see page 98), being careful not to catch the poppy fabric in the stitches.*

8 *Next fold in the backing fabric seam allowance, pin, then slip stitch. Be sure that the backing stitches do not catch the wadding near the edges of the blocks.*

Join the long strips together, using the same method.

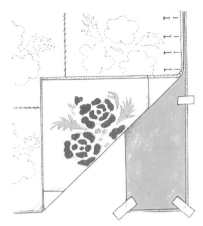

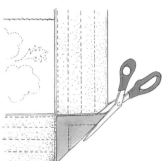

11 *(Left). Lay the quilt right side down on a table and fold the quilted border back towards the seam. The corners will be bulky so trim away the corner triangle, before making a mitred corner (see page 103).*

12 *(Right). Turn in a seam allowance, tucking the wadding out of the way, pin then slip stitch.*

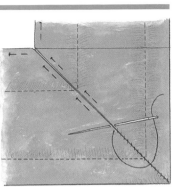

9 *Cut four borders 21.5cm (8¹/₂in) wide, two 191.5cm (75¹/₂in) long and two 193.5cm (76¹/₂in) long. Cut four strips of wadding the same size. Place a strip of wadding on a table with a border strip, placed right side up, on the top. Cover the wadding and border strip with the quilt, right side down, lining up the edges. Pin and repeat on the other side. Machine stitch, finger press open and repeat for the top and bottom of the quilt with the remaining border.*

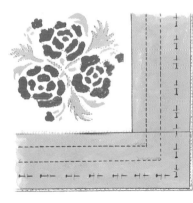

10 *Using a sliver of soap, mark three quilling lines 5cm (2in) apart along the borders. Pin tack with horizontal pins (see page 105). Machine quilt (see page 106).*

STENCILLED POPPY QUILT CHARTED TEMPLATE:
1 SQ = 5CM (2IN)

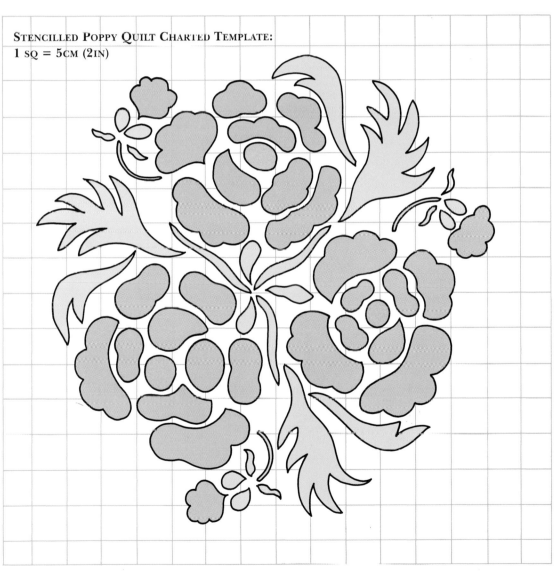

Dolly Mixtures

The colours of this baby quilt are taken from the sweets called Dolly Mixtures. Potatoes and a carrot are cut into shapes and then used as printing blocks with soft fabric paints. The template looks involved, but only needs to be drafted once. When the colours have been heat set with an iron, the quilt is fully washable. The finished size of the quilt is 100 x 70cm (39 x 28in).

DOLLY MIXTURES CHARTED TEMPLATE: 1 SQ = 5CM (2IN)

WORKBASKET
❖

1.6m (1³/₄yd) white cotton fabric 114cm (45in) wide.
❖

110 x 80cm (39 x 36in) wadding
❖

1 reel white cotton thread
❖

1 pot each of soft fabric paint in yellow, pink, green, and purple
❖

2 pots soft fabric paint in white
❖

3 large potatoes
❖

1 carrot
❖

Fine pencil
❖

Paintbrush
❖

Jam jar with water
❖

Saucer
❖

Craft knife
❖

Waterproof pen
❖

Kitchen roll
❖

Piece of plastic approximately 110 x 80cm (43 x 32in) (or open flat a large storage bag)
❖

2 pieces of felt or an old blanket 100 x 80cm (43 x 32in)
❖

Masking tape
❖

Template plastic or card
❖

Dressmaker's 5cm (2in) graphpaper

1 *Use the quarter template (right) and a waterproof pen to draw up the outer guidelines, the centre cross and the four diamond areas onto the dressmaker's graphpaper. Draw in one example each of the square triangle and diamond shapes and, using these as templates, trace out onto template plastic or card and cut out. Referring to the template and drawing around the triangle and square shapes, fill in the borders.*

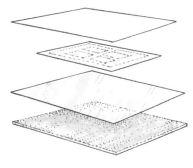

2 *Cut the white cotton fabric in half to make two pieces 103 x 73cm (41 x 30in) for the top and backing. Wash the fabric to remove the finish so that the printing will adhere, then press well. Use masking tape to attach a couple of large pieces of felt or an old blanket to a table and cover with a piece of plastic taped firmly in place. Tape the pattern guide to the plastic and, tape down the white fabric, making sure that there are no wrinkles in any of the layers. Use a fine pencil to rule in the three outside quilting lines.*

Use this quarter template to draw up the complete pattern onto white cotton fabric. When you have enlarged the square, triangle, and diamond shapes to their correct size, use them as templates to cut out printing blocks from old potatoes.

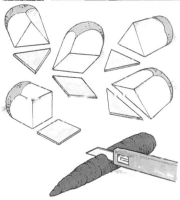

Continue to paint the block and print, cleaning up the edges of the block and washing the brush and your hands from time to time. When all the pink shapes are finished, mix 5ml (1tsp) of each of the remaining paints with 5ml (1tsp) of white paint. Print the remaining coloured shapes from the centre outwards until the printing is complete. Leave to dry. Following the manufacturer's instructions, press with a hot iron to set the colours.

3 Cut the potatoes in half and check that the templates will fit. Using a sharp craft knife, cut one printing block of each shape plus an extra triangle, making sure that you leave a good "handle" to grasp. The extra triangle is needed for the change in colour in case the first colour has stained the potato. Cut off the end of a carrot to create the circle shape for printing.

4 Mix 15ml (1tbsp) each of pink and white paint in a saucer. Have handy some kitchen paper to wipe up any drips. Before starting on the quilt, practise on a scrap of fabric. If you are happy with the result continue. Take the diamond potato block and, using a paintbrush, cover with pink paint. Press gently but firmly between the diamond guidelines and make one print.

Follow the instructions on page 104 for layering, then machine sew (see page 106) over the pencil lines and between the diamond shapes. Finish by following the binding instructions on pages 104–105.

Dyeing for Bed

A truly creative project in which you can hand dye fabric to your own choice of colours. No expensive equipment is needed and the speed with which the colour dyes the fabric can become addictive. Dye the fabric for the backing too for a quilt with a professional finish. When working with dyes, be sure to follow the manufacturer's instructions carefully. The finished size is 232 x 151cm (88 x 58in).

WORKBASKET

❖

6.5m (6¹/₂yd) white cotton sheeting which has been washed in hot water at 95 degrees with a mild soap powder

❖

25g (1oz) Procion dye in cerise, violet and golden yellow

❖

243 x 152cm (96 x 60in) wadding

❖

1 reel grey cotton thread for piecing

❖

1 reel mauve cotton thread for quilting

❖

3 or 4 catlitter trays

❖

1 large bucket

❖

Metal spoons for mixing dye

❖

Salt

❖

Urea crystals (for dissolving dye)

❖

Soda ash or soda crystals

❖

33cm (13in) square of card

1 Wash the fabric and tear into strips across the width. Tear three at 46cm (18in) (for colours A and C), two at 30cm (12in) (for colours B and D), one at 61cm (24in) (for colour E). Cut two strips down the length at 64cm (25in) (for colour F). The long strips will make the four borders.

Mix 8ml (1¹/₂ tsp) of cerise dye and 12.5ml (2¹/₂ tsp) of violet dye together with 45ml (3tbsp) urea (which helps the dye to dissolve) in a little bit of water. Add 350g (12oz) of salt dissolved in about 1 litre (2 pints) of boiling water. Use just enough water to dissolve the salt, the less water the more textured the result. Let the salt solution cool to warm, then add the dye mixture. Pour into a bucket and add one 30cm (12in) strip of fabric (colour D), ensuring the solution covers all the fabric, but moving it as little as possible to give texture. The colour is quite strong, so to achieve a lighter colour, either reduce the amount of dye or add more fabric. Leave the fabric for 10 minutes then add 45ml (3tbsp) of soda ash or soda crystals dissolved in about 1 litre (2 pints) of warm water.

Make the gradation for colour C by adding one 46cm (18in) length 10 minutes after the soda has been added. Press the scrunched up fabric against the dyed strip of fabric to "print" extra texture.

2 Wait another 10 minutes, then add the 61cm (24in) length for colour E. It is possible to achieve at least five colour gradations if the initial dye is dark. Leave the fabric in the dye for three hours and then rinse in cold running water. When the water is clear, wash in a washing machine in warm water and 15ml (1tbsp) of mild washing powder.

3 For a space-dyed or variegated effect in colour A, mix 1¹/₂tsp cerise red and 15ml (3tsp) golden yellow dye in separate containers with a warm salt only (no urea) solution of 350g (12oz) salt and 1 litre (2 pints) boiling water. Arrange two 46cm (18in) strips of fabric in two cat litter trays in a random manner. Spoon the red and then the yellow dye in rows over the fabric. Where the colours meet the dyes will make new colours. Wait 10 minutes and then add soda as in step 1.

4 Move the fabric about with your hands to mix the colours more – the divisions between the colours will blur. Wait 30 minutes, then rinse under cold running water. For colour B, add a 30cm (12in) strip to the remaining dye and leave for half an hour. Rinse till clear, then wash in a machine, using warm water and a mild washing powder.

Dyeing for Bed

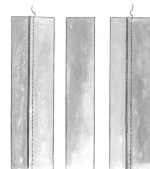

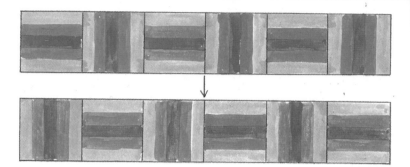

5 *For the borders, mix 8ml (1¹/₂tsp) cerise red and 8ml (1¹/₂tsp) violet dye in a warm salt only (no urea) solution of 350g (12oz) of salt and 1 litre (2 pints) boiling water. Arrange the two 64cm (25in) lengths in a large cat litter tray in rhythmic ripples. Lift the fabric away from one corner and pour in the dye mixture, allowing the dye to reach the fabric from the bottom of the tray and leaving the top of the fabric dry. Do not disturb for 30 minutes, then add the soda mixture as in step 1. Wait for 30 minutes, then push the top fabric down into the dye. The fabric at the bottom of the tray will dye in dark wrinkles and the rest will be a lighter colour. Leave the fabric in the dye for 30 more minutes before rinsing under cold running water. Rinse until clear and then wash as before. This will be colour F.*

6 *Using the rotary cutter (see page 99), cut four long strips 5cm (2in) wide across the width from colours B and E. From colour A cut two long strips 6.5cm (2¹/₂in) wide. Join, chain fashion (see page 100), right sides together, colours B and E, then add colour A. Press well. The strip should be 22.5cm (8¹/₂in) wide.*

7 *Using the rotary cutter, cut the strips into 12 22.5cm (8¹/₂in) squares (see page 99). Lay out the 12 squares, so that one square has the strips running across and the next with the strips running down. Join together, chain fashion, to make two strips of six squares each. Press the seams in opposite directions (see page 100). Join the two strips together as illustrated above.*

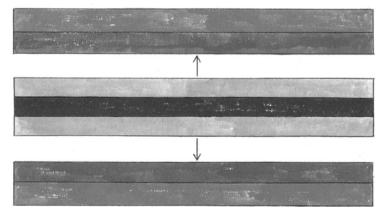

8 *Using the rotary cutter, from each of colours A, B and E cut two long strips 4cm (1¹/₂in) wide. From colour D cut one strip the same width. Join them together in the order shown to make a strip 19cm (7¹/₂in) wide.*

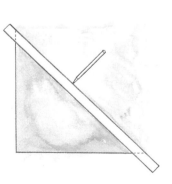

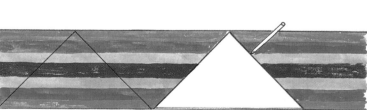

9 *To make a triangle template from card, measure two lines 27.5cm (10⁷/₈in) long at right angles and join to form a triangle. Cut out.*

10 *Place the template at the end of the strip on the wrong side, as shown. Using a sharp pencil, rule four triangles and cut out.*

11 *Use the same template to make four triangles from colour E. Join the plain and striped triangles to make four 27.5cm (10¹/₂in) squares.*

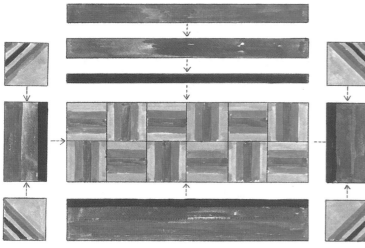

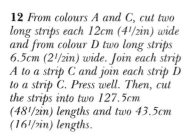

14 *Follow the instructions for sandwiching the quilt, wadding and backing layers together (see page 104) and pin tack (see page 105). Follow the quilting diagram to machine quilt methodically. Quilt all main horizontal lines first. Then quilt the centre line between the squares. Next quilt all the main vertical lines. Quilt the horizontal, diagonal and vertical lines circling the centre panel. Quilt all diagonal lines in the order shown. Finish off the loose ends on the back (page 106).*

Trim the edges of the quilt top straight (see page 102). Cut binding strips 4cm (1¹/₂in) wide from the fabric in colour A and attach as shown on pages 104–105.

12 *From colours A and C, cut two long strips each 12cm (4¹/₂in) wide and from colour D two long strips 6.5cm (2¹/₂in) wide. Join each strip A to a strip C and join each strip D to a strip C. Press well. Then, cut the strips into two 127.5cm (48¹/₂in) lengths and two 43.5cm (16¹/₂in) lengths.*

Next attach the long three-colour strips to either side of the centre panel. Press. Attach a square with diagonal stripes to either side of the two short three-colour strips. Press, then add to the main quilt, top and bottom. Press.

From colour F, cut two border strips 180.5 x 25.5cm (68¹/₂ x 10¹/₂in) long and two border strips 147.5 x 25.5cm (56¹/₂ x 10¹/₂in) long. Attach the longer strips to the sides of the quilt first, press, then lastly attach the shorter strips to the top and bottom of the quilt.

13 *Mark up the quilting lines as shown in step 14 (right), using a sliver of soap and a square quilter's rule for the borders.*

Painted Stripes

An adventurous way to design and print your own fabric is to use a small foam paint roller cut into narrow widths. Fabric paint comes in many beautiful colours and those given here could be substituted to co-ordinate with your furnishings. The finished size of this lap quilt is 100 x 85cm (40x35½in).

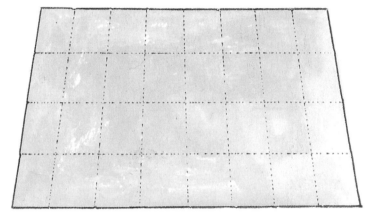

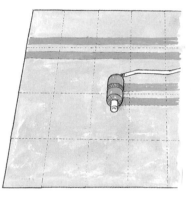

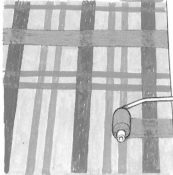

WORKBASKET

❖

1.8m (2yd) white or cream cotton fabric 114cm (45in) wide, cut into two pieces for the top and the backing

❖

100 x 90cm (40 x 36in) wadding

❖

1 reel cream cotton thread

❖

1 pot each of fabric paint in green, turquoise, yellow, blue

❖

2 pots soft fabric paint in white

❖

1 small roller and 2 sponge covers

❖

Paintbrush

❖

A large piece of plastic (split a plastic bag at the sides)

❖

Masking tape

❖

Jam jar of water

❖

Flat plate

❖

Hairdryer

1 *Press guidelines into one of the pieces of fabric, folding the fabric in half lengthways and folding in half again, so that three evenly spaced lines are pressed into the fabric. Repeat widthways, folding in half three times to make seven cross lines. Tape an old blanket or large piece of felt to a table, then cover with a piece of plastic slightly larger than the quilt fabric. Tape the fabric smoothly over the plastic.*

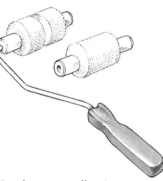

2 *Cut the sponge rollers into two 2.5cm (1in) widths and a 5cm (2in) width. The double rollers are used for the green and the yellow stripes. The single roller for the blue and turquoise stripes.*

3 *Pour the pot of yellow paint into a jam jar and add one third from one pot of the white paint. Mix well, then put some onto a large flat plate. Roll some paint onto the double roller, centre the roller over the centre fold and paint yellow strips either side of this fold. Paint with a firm but gentle touch, refilling the roller around halfway up the line. Any light patches can be touched in with the paintbrush. Repeat for the other two pressed lines. Use the 5cm (2in) roller to paint lines in blue paint (with a third of the white paint added) between and either side of the yellow lines. Leave the paint to dry thoroughly before adding the cross lines. A hairdryer will speed up the process. Meanwhile, wash and dry the sponge rollers. It is most important to let them dry thoroughly or the paint will bleed during the next application*

4 *Add one third of a pot of white paint to the green paint. Using the two 2.5cm (1in) sponges, paint lines either side of the centre and quarter lines as before. Add a third of a pot of the white paint to the turquoise and, using the 5cm (2in) sponge, paint lines between and either side of the green lines. Follow the manufacturer's instructions for setting the paint.*

Prepare for quilting according to the layering and pinning instructions on page 104. Quilt as shown in the main picture either side of the blue lines, and between the yellow and green double lines. Use a walking foot and toning cream thread, and use the side of the machine foot as a guide along the edges of the painted strips. Follow the instructions for binding a quilt, "Folding Towards the Back", on pages 104–105.

Double X (No.3)

Patchwork without piecing! Paint on silk and make this eyecatching wallhanging. The finished size of the wallhanging is 62 x 32cm (24½ x 12½in).

WORKBASKET
✤
80cm (1yd) medium weight haboutai silk 112cm (44in) wide, prewashed and pressed whilst still damp
✤
40cm (½yd) soft shape needlepunch wadding
✤
1 reel gold-coloured thread
✤
Silk paint in pink, blue, turquoise, rust and pale jade
✤
Medium-size paintbrush
✤
Tube of gold gutta
✤
Piece of firm pelmet interfacing 61 x 30cm (24 x 12in)
✤
1 packet tiny gold beads
✤
Gold tassel
✤
2 water jars
✤
Graphpaper
✤
Masking tape
✤
Fine pencil
✤
Silk pins
✤
Hairdryer if desired
✤
Kitchen roll
✤
4 corner blocks
✤
8 screws
✤
Fine sandpaper
✤
Drill

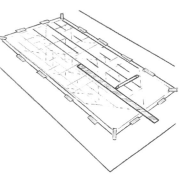

1 *Transfer the template opposite onto 5cm (2in) dressmaker's graphpaper as shown on page 97. Cut or tear the silk into two 70 x 40cm (28 x 16in) sized pieces.*

Using masking tape, attach the design to a white surface or over paper on a table. Tape one piece of the silk over the top, making sure that the design is centred, the grain is straight and the silk is held firmly. Using a fine pencil, trace over the design, ruling the vertical lines first, then the horizontal and finally the diagonal. Check that all the lines have been drawn. The lines will be covered by the gold gutta.

DOUBLE X (NO. 3) CHARTED TEMPLATE: 1 SQ = 4CM (1½IN)

2 *Pin, using silk pins, or tape the silk to a frame (see page 107). Make sure the fabric is taut. Next, apply gold gutta over the vertical lines, starting in the centre and working towards the edge. Turn the piece and work the rest of the vertical lines from the opposite side. It is important to apply the gutta lines in one direction only and then leave to dry or they will smudge. If you wish to speed up the drying process you can use a hairdryer. The*

horizontal lines are easier to draw if you rest your hand on a piece of wood placed across the frame.

When the horizontal lines are finished leave them to dry before applying the diagonal lines, again using the length of wood to prevent smudging. Check there are no gaps in the gutta by holding the work up to the window and fill in any spaces. Otherwise, the paint will run through holes into the next shape.

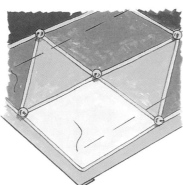

3 *Once you are sure the gutta is dry and referring to the template, start to paint one colour at a time. Shake each paint pot before using, and stand it about 30cm (12in) away from the work as the tiny bubbles tend to splash. Place the paint pot on some kitchen roll and keep a piece of kitchen roll in your spare hand to dry the brush. Be sure to wash the brush well between applications and frequently check your hands are clean. When all the shapes have been painted, run some turquoise colour outside the edging line. Leave to dry before removing it from the frame. Follow the manufacturer's instructions for heat setting the paint. Press a fold line 6mm (scant ¹/₄in) outside the gutta line.*

4 *Cut the wadding 6mm (¹/₄in) larger than the diagram and centre the silk painting. Fold the edges of the silk to the back and hold in place with pins. Tack the silk to the wadding, using silk thread if possible, as it will not make holes in the fabric. Sew gold beads onto the points of the stars, working a double stitch and running the sewing thread along the back of the work between beads.*

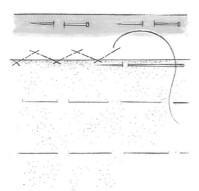

5 *When the beading is finished, pin the excess silk fabric to the back of the piece, turning under a small hem. Sew using a herringbone stitch (see page 98).*

6 *Make a backing from pelmet interlining, cut slightly smaller than the wallhanging. Cut a hanging sleeve 9cm (3¹/₂in) wide, press in a seam allowance on all sides and machine stitch to the top (straight edge) of the interfacing. Pin the backing in place and slip stitch. Finish by sewing a purchased tassel onto the point of the wallhanging.*

Appliquéd Quilts

The versatility of appliqué is seen in this chapter, with a choice of five very individual quilts. Hand and machine sewn, there are large and small projects ranging from traditional to contemporary.

Art Nouveau

The peacock feather fabric used in this Art Nouveau-inspired quilt was designed in 1887 and the appliqué shape taken from a picture frame of the same period. The stylized roses and frame are worked before quilting to make an elegant single quilt. Machine-sewn contour quilting is used both inside and outside the frame. A wide binding in the peacock design fabric finishes this handsome quilt. Its finished size is 225 x 152cm (89 x 60in).

WORKBASKET
❖

2m (2yd) patterned lawn cotton fabric in mauve 90cm (36in) wide

❖

5m (5yd) mauve background fabric 114cm (45in) wide

❖

5 pieces of cotton fabric 30cm (12in) square in 2 deep, 1 medium and 1 light toning pinks, and 1 purple colour

❖

2.4m (2½yd) cotton backing fabric 152cm (60in) wide

❖

243 x 152cm (96 x 60in) wadding

❖

2m (2¼yd) ultra fine, iron-on interfacing

❖

3 reels grey cotton thread

❖

1 reel neutral cotton thread

❖

4 reels of cotton thread to match the fabric for the roses

❖

Clear or open embroidery foot

❖

2 sheets template plastic 30cm (12in) square

❖

Waterproof pen

❖

Double-sided sticky tape

❖

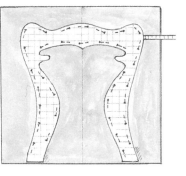

1 *Enlarge the template on page 55 to measure 193 x 89cm (76 x 35in), either using a photocopier or onto dressmaker's graphpaper, following the method shown on page 97. Cut out the "frame" along the inner and outer lines. Trace the centre flower and one of the smaller flowers onto template plastic using a waterproof pen, and number each petal.*

Cut the background fabric in half across the width, and lightly press a guideline lengthways down the centre of one piece. Fold the fabric in half, right sides together. Centre the frame template on the fabric, lining up the marked foldline with the fold of the fabric. Pin to the fabric. Using a fine pencil, draw around both sides of the template. Unpin the template and repeat on the other side of the fabric, matching the frame at the foldline. Unfold the fabric. Using the flowers enlarged onto photocopy or graphpaper, position the three smaller flowers as shown in the guide, and trace the flower stems through onto the wrong side of the fabric, either by taping the fabric to a window or by using a

light box. Hold the flower templates in place with pins or double-sided sticky tape, but do not leave the tape on the fabric for longer than a few minutes. Position the large flower in the centre and trace onto the fabric in the same way.

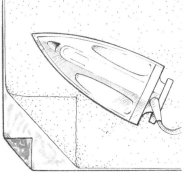

2 *Press ultra fine, iron-on interfacing to the wrong side of the patterned lawn cotton fabric. Be sure to press rather than iron so that the interfacing remains smooth. Use a dry, warm iron to start with, and when the whole piece is attached, turn it over and press the right side with a steam iron. Place the patterned fabric right side down on a table and centre the background fabric over it so that the drawn design is right side up.*

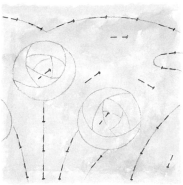

3 *Pin along the pencil lines, ensuring that the two layers remain smooth. Put plenty of pins in the spaces to stabilize the fabric so that it does not move during machining. If possible use a clear or open embroidery foot on the sewing machine. Fill the bobbin with thread, which should match the patterned fabric. Using a small zig-zag width 1, stitch length 1, or a straight stitch length 1, sew along the edges of the drawn lines of the "frame". Next sew along the lines of the flower stems, using the width of the machine foot as a guide for the second line of stitches.*

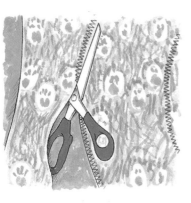

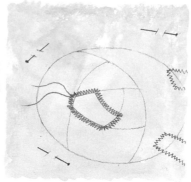

4 *Turn the fabric over and trim as closely as possible to the machine lines, protecting the background fabric with your fingers underneath. Tilt the scissors, holding the blades flat. First cut away the frame, then around the flower stems. Do not worry if the odd stitch is cut – it will be covered by the satin stitch later. Press well.*

5 *The appliqué flower petals are also cut to shape after each one has been attached, in sequence, to the background fabric.*

Cut a piece of deep pink fabric to cover template 1 and pin it on the right side of the main background fabric over the drawn flower. As the flower is drawn on the back it will be necessary to flop the fabric over to check it is in the right place. Repeat for all four flowers.

6 *Working from the wrong side, sew around and just outside the drawn line, using a small zig-zag stitch. Start by bringing the bobbin thread up to the wrong side of the work and hold the ends as you start to sew. This will avoid knots appearing on the right side. Start sewing each petal just short of where the next line will be sewing. Turn to the right side and trim as closely as possible to the stitching. These small stitches will be covered later by satin stitch.*

7 *Next, position pieces of the second deep pink fabric (template 2) as before. Working on the wrong side, stitch in place, but this time where the two fabrics overlap sew exactly on the line. This will prevent too much bulk from build-up of stitches. Trim as before.*

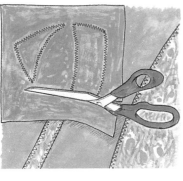

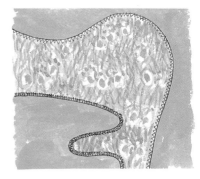

8 *Continue sewing and trimming each petal. When sewing two petals of the same colour onto one flower, cut enough fabric to cover both and sew at the same time. Press.*

9 *Before starting the appliqué satin stitch, fill the bobbin with a neutral colour thread. Depending on your machine either thread the lower tension, tighten the bobbin case a little, or loosen the top tension slightly. The lower tension will now be slightly tight, which will avoid bobbin stitches showing on the top, a neat round stitch will be formed on the right side of the quilt.*

To prevent puckers on finer fabrics, it is advisable to use thin typing paper or one of the various special tearaway products under the work. This is torn away when the stitching is completed.

Set the machine to satin stitch width 2–3. Work a practice flower using similar scraps of fabric. Start from the centre with thread matching the first deep pink colour, and continue changing the top thread to match the petals. Satin stitch over each line, following the order shown on the template opposite. Stitch around petals 6 and 7 as shown. Work each line of stitching so that the ends of the previous line are covered. A space-dyed thread saves time changing different threads.

If the fabric sticks as the foot crosses a previous line of satin stitch, tuck a piece of folded paper under the back of the foot to bring the work forward.

10 *Using grey thread, satin stitch around the inside of the frame. The outside is sewn in with the wadding. Press well from the wrong side.*

Cut two long strips 23cm (9in) wide from the remaining piece of background fabric. Pin then sew them, right sides together, either side of the appliqué frame. Press.

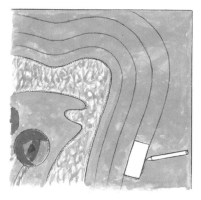

11 *Mark up for quilting by cutting pieces of thin card to the required width and running them along the outside of the frame, marking a line with a piece of soap or quilter's pencil. The lines should be 4cm, 6cm, 7cm, 8cm, 9cm, 10cm, 12cm (1½, 2½, 2½, 2¾, 3, 3¼in) apart. If your walking foot takes a quilting guide there is no need to mark quilting lines. Draw in the centre quilting details.*

Layer the backing fabric, the wadding and the top fabric and pin tack on the quilting lines (see pages 104–105). Using a walking foot, work the quilting lines outside the frame first, so that the pins can be removed. Sew a line of straight stitch around the edge of the frame. Fill in the centre quilting lines, working the tight curves a few stitches at a time and leaving the needle in the down position whilst turning the quilt. Lastly, work the outside of the frame with satin stitch. Measure and trim the edges (see page 102).

The wide binding can be made from offcuts from the centre. Tear off the interfacing, and cut strips 2.5cm (2in) wide. Join, checking the pattern runs the same way. Measure then pin the binding, setting it in 1.5cm (½in) from the sides (see page 105). Attach to the quilt and slip stitch to the back.

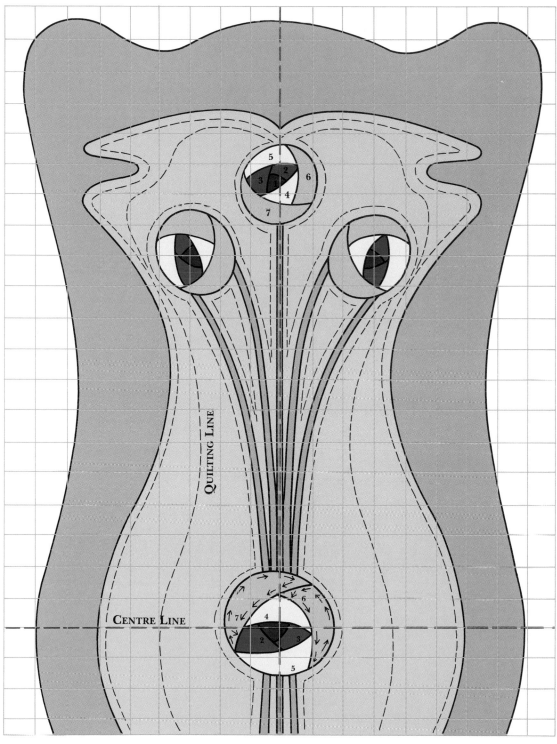

QUILTING LINE

CENTRE LINE

Ring-a-Roses

Ideal for quilters who find flowers difficult to draw, this cot quilt features floral designs cut from lightweight furnishing fabrics. A wide range of remnants and samples featuring flowers can be obtained very cheaply from soft furnishing stores, giving flower arrangers the opportunity to be wonderfully creative with fabric. The roses used here would welcome to the world a June baby, but other appropriate flowers would look as attractive. The finished size of the quilt is 108 x 81cm (42¹/₂ x 32in).

WORKBASKET
❖
80cm (1yd) cotton fabric 114cm (45in) wide for the background
❖
90cm (1yd) cotton backing fabric 114cm (45in) wide
❖
25cm (¹/₄yd) red cotton fabric 114cm (45in) wide
❖
25cm (¹/₄yd) green cotton fabric 114cm (45in) wide
❖
110 x 90cm (45 x 39in) wadding
❖
1 reel spaced-dyed machine embroidery thread to match the flowers
❖
1 reel neutral thread for the background
❖
Several pieces of lightweight, flowered furnishing fabric, enough to yield about 28 medium-sized flowers, some leaves, rosebuds and 4 large feature flowers for the corners
❖
1m (1yd) bonding paper
❖
Thin typing paper

1 *Using a steam iron, press pieces of bonding web onto the back of the chosen flowers and leaves. Select more flowers than needed for a good selection for the arrangement.*

From the background fabric, cut a 47.5cm (18¹/₂in) square, two side panels 104.5 x 14cm (43¹/₂ x 5¹/₂in) and two top and bottom panels

53.5x 27cm (20¹/₂ x 11¹/₂in). From each of the red and green fabrics cut four strips 3cm (1in) wide. Cut five strips from both colours 4cm (1¹/₂in) wide. These form the borders and may need joining (see step 4).

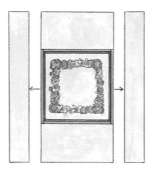

4 *Measure and cut two of the 3cm (1in) wide red strips to fit the top and bottom edges of the appliqué square. Sew in place and press after every addition in this step. Measure and cut the other two strips to fit the sides and attach in the same way. Continue measuring, cutting and sewing the four green strips in the same order. Add the top and bottom background panels and the side panels. Measure and add the red then the green border strips.*

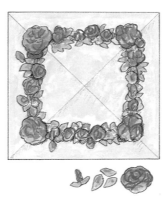

2 *Carefully cut out the flowers and peel off the backing paper. Fold the background square across both diagonals and lightly press in the two lines to use as a guide. Place the flowers in a square wreath arrangement onto the background fabric, keeping the flowers about 4cm (1¹/₂in) from the edge. Experiment by adding and subtracting leaves. When satisfied, carefully press the flowers in place.*

5 *Bond the four feature flowers to each corner of the quilt and satin stitch around the edges as above. Pull through any loose threads and tie at the back. Press well.*

3 *Use a clear appliqué or open embroidery foot to sew the flowers in place. Set the machine to a narrow satin stitch. Fill the bobbin with a neutral colour thread. Refer to your machine manual to tighten the lower tension. This will prevent the bobbin thread showing on the top and a neat, round stitch will be formed on the quilt top. Work a test flower on some spare fabric. Place thin typing paper or a special tearaway product under the fabric while you work – this will help to keep the background fabric flat. The paper is torn away after the appliqué is finished. Sew satin stitch around the edges of the rosebuds first, then the flowers in each corner, then the remainder of the flowers. These last flowers can be stitched with the space-dyed thread and should cover all the end threads from the previous stitching. Press from the wrong side. Check the piece is square and trim to 47.5cm (18¹/₂in).*

6 *On a piece of paper, draw a freehand curved quilting guide-line. Measure and draw a parallel line 3cm (1¹/8in) away and cut out the curved strip on the lines. Pin the paper to the quilt top and draw around either side with a fine pencil.*

Sandwich the top, wadding and backing fabric together, following the instructions on pages 104–105, and pin tack (see page 105). Quilt the centre motif first, then, dropping the feed dog, outline both the outer and inner edges of the rose wreath, sewing close to the satin stitching. Use the walking foot to work the curved quilting, then change the top thread to that matching the flowers and machine quilt (see page 106) between the narrow red and green strips, around the rose wreath and either side of the red border.

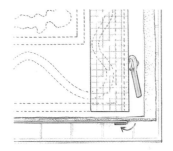

7 *To trim the excess wadding and backing accurately from the edges, place the quilt right side down on a cutting board and tuck the green border under, well away from the edge. Use the quilting line as a guide and cut 1.5cm (¹/2in) from it with the rotary cutter. Bind by turning the green strip to the back (see pages 104–105).*

On the Beach

Made from felt, this piece would remind children of happy seaside memories. The simple shapes are quickly appliquéd by hand using a running stitch, and as felt does not fray, it is not necessary to turn under the edges. The hands and footsteps in the sand were made by drawing around children's hands and feet, but templates are provided if you need them. The templates are shown in reverse so that after tracing onto bonding paper, the image will appear the correct way round. The finished quilt measures 94 x 64cm (37 x 27in).

WORKBASKET
❖

Felt craft squares in blue x 2, green x 2, orange x 1, pink x 1, bright pink x 1, flesh x 1, white x 1, pale blue x 1

❖

25cm (9in) each of lavender and turquoise felt

❖

60cm (2/3yd) bright yellow felt

❖

25cm (1/4yd) pale yellow felt

❖

90cm (1yd) red felt 183cm (72in) wide to use for backing

❖

Fine embroidery thread to match or contrast with the felt

❖

50cm (1/2yd) fusible bonding paper

❖

Strip of iron-on interfacing 94 x 5cm (37¹/2 x 2in)

❖

Dressmaker's 5cm (2in) graphpaper

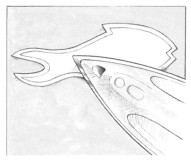

1 *Following the measurements below, which include seam allowances of 7.5mm (¹/4in), cut the background shapes from felt. Sew the skyline over the sea for the background to the boat. Enlarge the templates on pages 60–61 as shown on page 97. Trace onto the smooth side of the bonding paper. Cut out just outside the drawn line. With a steam iron, press the shapes onto the appropriate coloured pieces of felt, keeping the drawn lines uppermost. Leave to cool, then cut out the motifs on the drawn line, peel off the backing paper, centre and press them onto the right side of the backgrounds.*

Sew the motifs to the background shapes with a running stitch (see page 98) along the edges of each one, using matching or contrasting threads. The motif details will be quilted after the backing has been added. When the motifs have been applied, join the background shapes together to make lengthways strips (see page 60), taking a 7.5mm (¹/4in) seam allowance. Press the seams open. Join the strips together, matching the corners of the squares. Add the hands and feet strips. Press and trim the edges to measure 91.5 x 59.5cm (35¹/2 x 23¹/2in).

2 *Cut four strips of red felt, two 91.5 x 6cm (35¹/2 x 2¹/2in) and two 69 x 6cm (27 x 2¹/2in). Sew the longer borders to the top and bottom first, then the remaining two to each side. Press. Cut the backing felt to fit. Cut a length of iron-on interfacing 97 x 5cm (37¹/2 x 2in) and, using a steam iron, attach it to the top border, setting it just short of the edge. This supports the hanging sleeve as no wadding is used.*

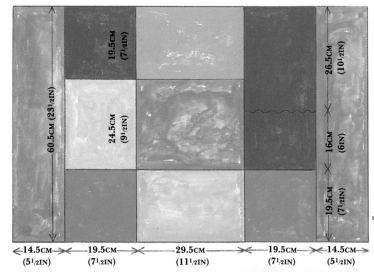

3 *Cut a hanging sleeve 10cm (4in) wide to fit just short of the width of the quilt. Sew a narrow seam allowance at each end and press in the seam allowance on one of the long sides. Set the sleeve 5.5cm (2¹/₄in) down from the top of the backing felt, right sides together, and machine stitch.*

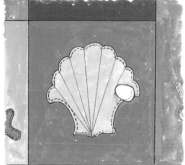

4 *Pin tack the backing felt and appliqué quilt together, matching the edges and checking that the hanging sleeve is at the top. Tie knots (see page 107) at the junctions where the background squares and rectangles meet to attach the backing to the quilt top. Use a sliver of soap to mark details such as the sea waves, sun rays, sand markings, seagull's wings, shell and ice cream. Quilt each panel and around the edges with a running stitch (see page 98). Sew on small circles of felt as the crab's eyes and fish bubbles.*

Slip stitch the hanging sleeve along the folded edge.

On the Beach

PIECING DIAGRAM

ON THE BEACH CHARTED TEMPLATES: 1 SQ = 5CM (2IN)

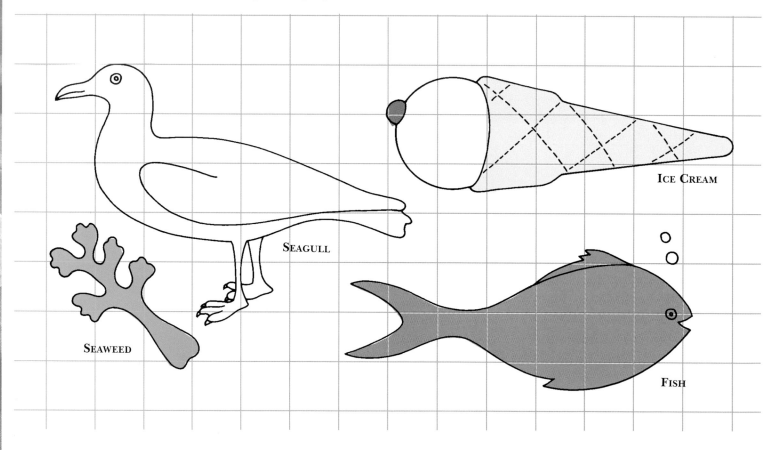

SEAGULL

ICE CREAM

SEAWEED

FISH

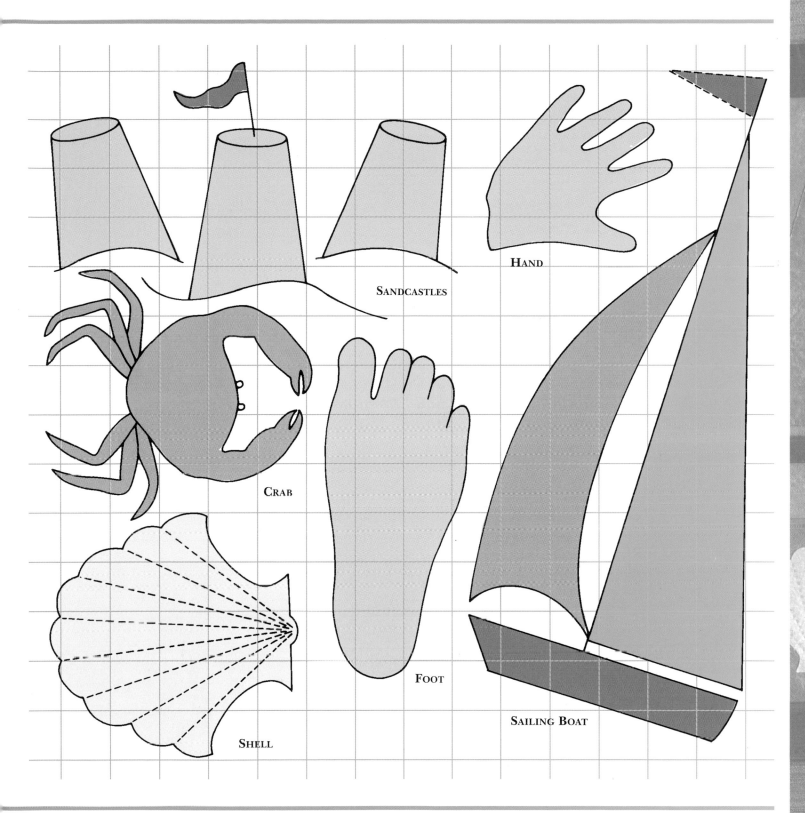

SANDCASTLES

HAND

CRAB

FOOT

SHELL

SAILING BOAT

Ribbon Knot Garden

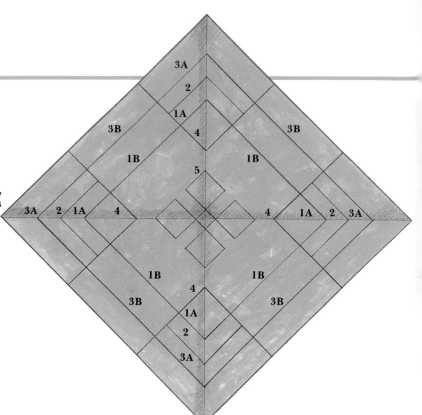

An unusual and creative way to use satin and jacquard ribbons can be seen to great effect on this beautiful bed quilt. This quilt would be more suitable for the more experienced quilter, although the design motif in the centre would make a good practice piece on a smaller cot quilt. Try a couple of mitred corners before you start. Sufficient ribbon is allowed for you to practice. The quilt is worked in sections to make handling easier, with the centre quilt worked before the borders and final ribbons are added. The finished quilt measures 204cm (82in) square.

WORKBASKET
❖

4.8m (5yd) green cotton fabric
114cm (45in) wide
❖

4.8m (5yd) cotton backing fabric
114cm (45in) wide
❖

214cm (86in) square wadding
❖

18m (20yd) pink jacquard ribbon
4cm (1½in) wide
❖

7m (8yd) pink jacquard ribbon
12mm (½in) wide
❖

8m (8½yd) yellow satin ribbon
2cm (1¾in) wide
❖

2m (2½yd) pink satin ribbon 2cm
(1¾in) wide
❖

Yellow and pink fine or machine
embroidery thread for sewing
the ribbons
❖

2 reels green cotton thread for
machine piecing and quilting

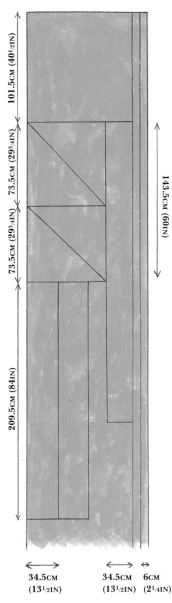

101.5CM (40½IN)

73.5CM (29¾IN)

73.5CM (29¾IN)

209.5CM (84IN)

143.5CM (60IN)

34.5CM
(13½IN)

34.5CM
(13½IN)

6CM
(2¼IN)

1 *Working from the cutting guide (right), cut both the green and the backing fabric as follows. Cut the 101.5cm (40½in) centre square, two 73.5cm (29¾in) squares, cut diagonally to make four triangles, and four borders, two 143.5 x 34.5cm (57½ x 13½in) and two 209.5 x 34.5cm (84 x 13½in) wide. Cut binding lengths 4cm (1½in) wide. The pieces will form the quilt top and backing.*

2 *Gently press diagonal folds from corner to corner on the large square. Measure down the diagonal lines 18cm (7in) and 37cm (14½in) from each corner and mark with a sliver of soap. Rule lines between those points to make two large inner squares. Next measure and make a* mark 28cm (11in) down the diagonal lines and, using a quilter's rule or set square, mark a square at each corner. Finally, using the diagonal lines as a guide, draw in the centre motif, a 24cm (10in) square with four 10cm (4in) squares in each corner.

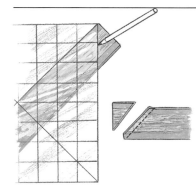

3 *Cutting four lengths for each measurement, from the wide jacquard ribbon cut lengths 68cm (27in), 185cm (73½in), 144cm (57½in) and 34cm (13½in) long. From the narrow jacquard ribbon cut lengths 16cm (6½in), 100cm* (40in), 33cm (13in) and 25cm (10in) long. From the yellow satin ribbon cut lengths 42cm (16½in), 33cm (13in), 60cm (23½in) and 48cm (19in) long. From the pink satin ribbon cut four 46cm (18in) lengths.

Group the ribbons together in matching lengths and pin a scrap of paper to each group giving the appropriate length. The mitred corners are sewn chain fashion (see page 100). Fold the ribbon, right sides together and, using a diagonal square as a guide, mark the sewing line with a white pencil. Sew, trim and press the seam allowance open as shown in the diagram. Be sure not to have the iron too hot.

Ribbon Knot Garden

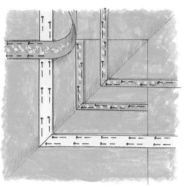

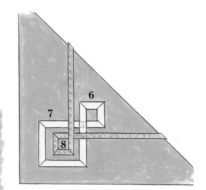

4 *Place the ribbons on the inside of the marked lines in the order given below. Pin and sew each ribbon on the stitching lines close to the edge before positioning the next type of ribbon. Position the ends of each ribbon at the points where they will be hidden by the next piece of ribbon to be laid over them. Sew both sides of the ribbon in the same direction. Place and sew the 16cm and 33cm (6¹/2in and 13in) narrow pink jacquard ribbon on the lines of the large, inner square (1A and 1B respectively). Sew the 25cm (10in) lengths on the right angles (2). Position and sew the 42cm and 33cm (16¹/2 and 13in) yellow satin ribbon on the large outer square (3A and 3B respectively). Sew the wide 68cm (27in) long jacquard ribbon on the outer right angles (4).*

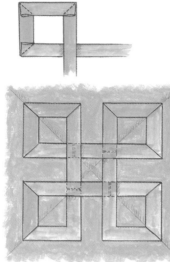

5 *Map out the positions of the 46cm (18in) pink satin ribbon lengths on the centre square (5), using the chalked lines on the outside edge of the ribbons. Make the first mitre's inner turn 14cm (5¹/2in) from the end of the ribbon. The second mitre's inner turn should be 5.5cm (2¹/4in) along and there should be a tail of 7cm (3³/4in) after the third mitre. Position the squares so that they weave under and over each other, making sure all the ends are covered. Pin and sew.*

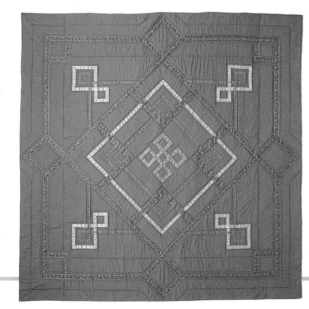

6 *Fold the green fabric triangles in half diagonally and gently press in a guide line. Work as in step 2, measuring from the corner of the triangle inside the seam allowance 7.5mm (¹/4in) from the edge. For the large yellow square (7) measure 9cm (3¹/2in) down the guideline and mark with a sliver of soap or a fine quilter's pencil a 17cm (6³/4in) square with the diagonal guide running from corner to corner. Draw the small yellow square (6) by measuring 30cm (11³/4in) along the diagonal fold and marking a 10cm (4in) square. Extend the ends of these two squares to meet up. The small pink square (8) will cover the ends of the yellow ribbon. Measure 15cm (6in) down the diagonal fold and make an 8cm (3in) square, extending the lines to run off the long side of the triangle.*

Take the 48cm (19in) and 60cm (23¹/2in) yellow satin ribbon lengths and and fold them in half and chain mitre. Make two more mitres either side with the outer measurements 10cm (4in) on the shorter lengths (6) and 17cm (6³/4in) on the longer lengths (7). Position and sew on the inside of lines 6 and 7 respectively, making sure the ends butt together. Work the 100cm (40in) length of narrow pink jacquard in the same way, mitring the ribbon at its centre and with the outer edge mitres formed 8cm (3in) from the first, centre mitre. The jacquard ribbon should cover the cut edges of the yellow ribbon and extend to the long sides of the triangle.

7 *Attach the long sides of the triangles to make a larger square of 143.5cm (60in). Press well on the wrong side of the fabric.*

Make the backing by joining the backing triangles to the large backing square as described above for the quilt top. Press. Place the backing on a table wrong side up and hold in place with masking tape. Centre the wadding over the backing, then lay the quilt on the top. The borders are added later. Run a tacking stitch along the seam line between the triangles and square. Pin tack all over (see page 105).

Machine quilt (see page 106) either side of each length of ribbon, using the side of the walking foot against the ribbon as a guide. To pivot at the corners, leave the needle in position in the quilt, lift the presser foot and turn the quilt at right angles before lowering the presser foot to continue sewing (see page 107). When all the quilting is complete, check the corners are square. If necessary, use a quilter's rule or a large set square and mark with soap before trimming with scissors (see page 102).

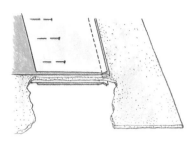

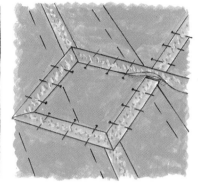

drawn line and overlapping onto the main quilt by 2.5cm (1in).

Fold the 34cm (13^1/$_2$in) lengths of jacquard ribbons in half and mitre. Position on the outside of the inner right angles of the four corner squares. Pin and sew in place. Fold the 144cm (57^1/$_2$in) jacquard ribbons in half and mitre. Attach to the long right angles at each corner in the same way, covering the ends of the previous ribbon sewed. The 185cm (73^1/$_2$in) jacquard ribbon lengths, will run diagonally over the seam lines between the centre square and the triangles into the border. Make the first mitre inside measurement 18cm (7in) from one end. Make the second and third mitres 15.5 (6in) apart. Pin the long sections in place on the outside lines of the centre border squares, tucking in the ends of the ribbons under the bottom points and, putting in plenty of pins, with extra pins added at the junctions. Machine stitch in place.

8 *Place the shorter border edges, right sides together, on the ends of the sides you have chosen as top and bottom, matching the edges. Tack in place. Turn the quilt over and pin the matching backing border lengths in the same way, sandwiching the wadding. Pin the borders on both sides out of the way and machine sew from the back.*

9 *Turn the quilt over and flop the borders over the wadding. Making sure the backing is flat, pin tack along the join, halfway down the borders, and along the edge. Next add the long borders in the same way. At this stage it is better to hand tack rather than to pin tack the three layers of the border together.*

10 *This step sees the final ribbon lengths attached, covering up the seam lines where the centre square and corner triangles were joined and the remainder of the ribbon ends. With a sliver of soap, rule a line all the way round the border 15cm (6in) from the seam line. Draw an 18cm (7in) square in each corner, within this square. Draw four 20cm (8in) squares in the centre of each border, with the points of the square lining up with the*

11 *Add the final quilting lines as shown in the diagram. Use the ribbon edge as a guide, and if there is not a quilting guide on the walking foot, use soap to rule in the extra lines.*

To finish, take out the tacking stitches and trim the edges straight with a rotary cutter, board and rule (see page 99). Attach the binding strips (see pages 104–105), turning the binding towards the back, and slip stitch in place.

Kandinski

An arrangement of exuberant geometric shapes cut from satin, silk and organza scraps gives this lively wallhanging a spontaneous feel, rather like the work of the Russian artist, Kandinski. The shapes are applied with bonding paper and machine stitching. The finished size is 63cm (25in) square.

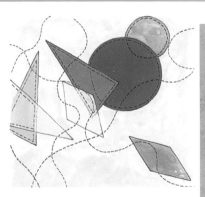

WORKBASKET

❖

40cm (16in) square of light grey dupion silk for the background

❖

60cm (²/₃yd) turquoise dupion silk or satin fabric 114cm (45in) wide for the frame

❖

1.2m (1¹/₄yd) flat domette

❖

1 reel pink rayon machine embroidery thread

❖

Scraps of brightly coloured silk, satin and organza

❖

50cm (¹/₂yd) paper-backed bonding web

2 *Gather together lots of scraps of brightly coloured silks and satins and press. Select the most pleasing arrangement of colours and press the bonding paper shapes onto the back of the silks, but not the organza as those shapes will only be held by a few stitches. Allow to cool and cut out on the line. Cut out the organza shapes, using a rotary cutter and mat (see page 99).*

1 *Draw your own simple shapes onto bonding paper, remembering that the image will appear in reverse. The shapes are a mixture of bonded and freely sewn pieces of organza, satin and silk, which are cut on the cross (bias) grain of the fabric to minimize fraying. Draw out more shapes than you need, so that there are plenty to choose from. Cut out the shapes just outside the drawn line.*

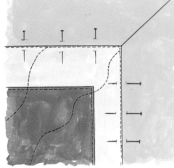

3 *Play with all the shapes until you have an arrangement you like, then remove the pieces which are to remain loose, and bond the others onto the grey silk using a steam iron. Keep the iron away from the organza as it has a tendency to melt!*

4 *Cut a square of domette 41cm (16in), place the silk over it and pin tack (see page 105). Machine straight stitch around the squares, circles and some of the triangles. Mark and then start to stitch some wavy lines. Sew the circles slowly, gently turning the work after every couple of stitches. Pull the threads to the back and knot (see page 106). Next, pin the organza and crêpe de chine shapes onto the fabric. Machine wavy lines over the organza shapes to hold them in place. Trim to 39.5cm (15¹/₂in).*

5 *Cut four borders from the frame silk 66 x 15cm (26 x 6in). Attach the borders to the main work, making mitred corners as shown on pages 104–105. Press.*

Cut a backing square of domette 63cm (25in). Place the work, right side down, on a flat surface and pin the domette to it, making sure it is square. The silk edges should overlap as they will be folded to the back as a

binding. Pin, then machine around the appliqué square "in the ditch" (see page 106), that is, close to the seam between the border and the appliqué. The stitching should hardly show. Pull the threads to the back and knot as before.

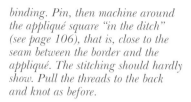

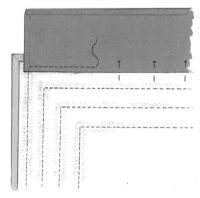

6 *Pin the overlapping silk edges to the back and slip stitch in place. On the right side, measure quilting lines from the centre out and mark with a sliver of soap 4cm, 3cm, 3cm, 1.5cm, 1.5cm (1½, 1¼, 1¼, ½, ½in). Pin tack across the marked lines (see page 105). Cut a hanging sleeve 62 x 11cm (24½ x 4½in). Turn in a seam at each end of the hanging sleeve and press a seam allowance in along one long side (see page 107).*

Machine quilt (see page 106), starting from the inside line, pivoting (see page 107) at the mitred corners. On the final line, pin the hanging sleeve on the back as shown in the diagram, so that it is sewn in the last round of quilting. Add a couple of extra curved quilting lines to hold the backing in place. Fold the hanging sleeve in place and slip stitch.

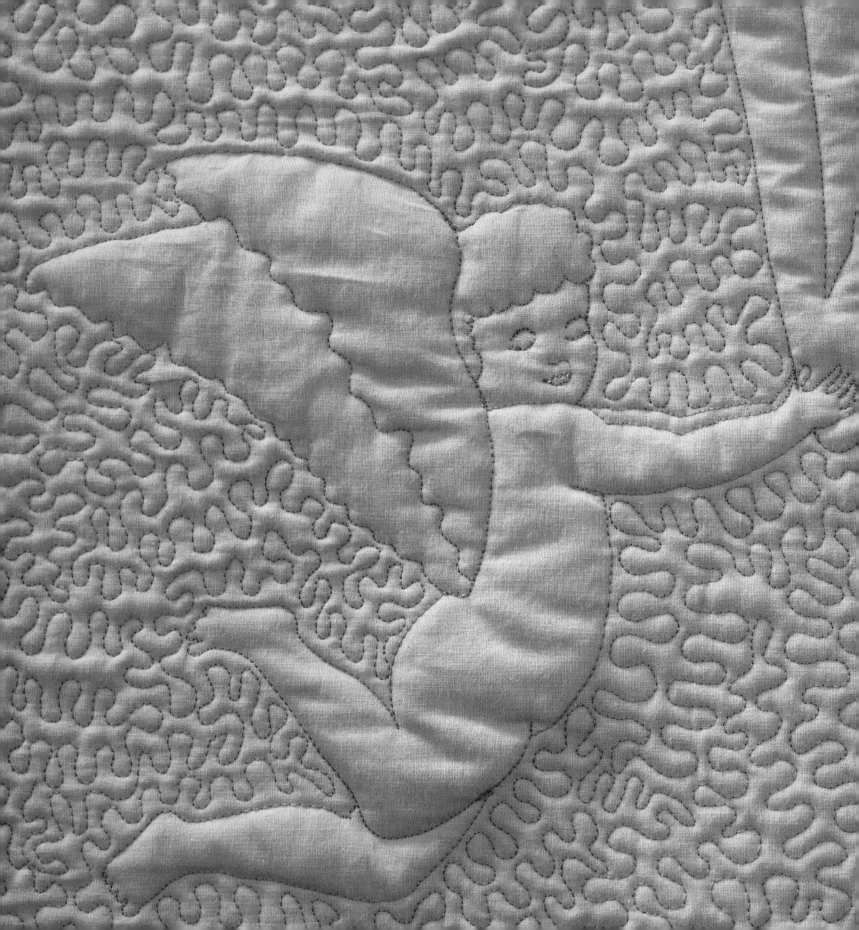

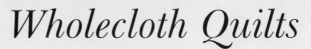

Wholecloth Quilts

Wholecloth quilts usually consist of one fabric embellished with stitched lines, which form intricate designs. We show shortcuts in five quilts to suit all ages and tastes.

Strippy Quilt

In years gone by, a traditional strippy quilt would have taken hours of quilting. This quilt is a modern interpretation, using the sewing machine for quick results. Choose a fabric with either a traditional or modern design featuring stripes of varying widths. One length of furnishing fabric is wide enough to cover a single bed, with the addition of co-ordinating borders. These can be cut wider, depending on the "drop" required. The finished quilt measures 239 x 165cm (94 x 65in).

WORKBASKET

❖

2.2m (2¼yd) floral striped lightweight furnishing fabric 138cm (54in) wide

❖

2.2m (2¼yd) co-ordinating plain fabric 114 (45in) wide for the borders

❖

2.3m (2½yd) backing fabric 152cm (60in) wide

❖

249 x 162cm (98 x 64in) wadding

❖

2 reels toning cotton thread

❖

Purchased cable template to fit the width of the fabric stripes

❖

Fine quilter's pencil

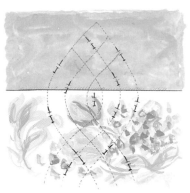

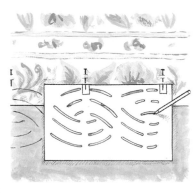

1 *Straighten the edges of the striped fabric (see page 102), which should be cut to 213cm (84in). Cut off the selvedge edges from both the main and border fabric.*

Cut four strips 17cm (6½in) wide from the border fabric, two 213cm (84in) long, two 169cm (66in) long. Join the strips onto the main fabric, sides first, then top and bottom (see pages 102–103). Press well. Attach register marks where the cable pattern repeats. Measure the quilting area length and divide the cable pattern measurement into the length. If there is not an exact division, it will be necessary to add or subtract a small amount from each space. Mark each division with a pin and stretch or shrink the lines slightly as the template is slid along during marking.

Mark the quilting lines onto the quilt top, using the cable template and a very fine quilter's pencil. Centre the cable template over the floral areas and half over the border. If you have straight lines in your fabric design, use them as a guide and quilt straight down without marking.

2 *The backing fabric may be slightly too narrow, therefore the borders have been cut wider so that they will fold back and cover the shortfall. Following the instructions for layering the quilt on page 106, prepare the backing, wadding and top for quilting. Pin, in the direction of machine quilting, along the outer lines of the cable, with a few in the centre to keep it from shifting, and along the printed straight lines of the fabric. The pins may be pulled out as the needle approaches each one.*

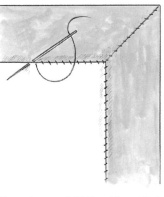

4 *Finger press a fold line 10cm (4in) from where the border joins the main quilt fabric and trim the wadding to this line. Fold the border to the back and mitre the corners. Turn under a seam allowance of 7.5mm (¼in) and pin to the backing. Slip stitch the border fabric to the quilt backing (see pages 102–103).*

3 *Machine quilt the straight lines first, so that those pins are removed. Sew a tiny back stitch at the end of each line, eliminating the need to tie off the ends. Machine quilt the cables, starting with the outer cable lines.*

Speedy Sashiko

Sashiko, a traditional Japanese quilting technique, is usually sewn by hand. The traditional quilting designs can be traced back many years when the large stitches were used as decoration as well as a way of prolonging the life of precious fabrics. This type of work is usually associated with coarsely woven indigo fabric and white stitches, but we have used luxury silk noil and buttonhole thread in unusual colours to make this lap quilt. Speedy machine techniques are used, working from the wrong side, with the buttonhole thread on the bobbin. The finished quilt measures 101 x 71cm (40 x 28in).

The Japanese love of asymetrical design is seen here with four traditional patterns: Seven Treasures of Buddha (centre), Fish Scales (bottom), The Plover Design (right), and A Stepped Design (left). Japanese quilted clothing was usually made without wadding, the stitched coarse spun indigo giving garments enough warmth for farmers and fishermen.

WORKBASKET

❖

80cm (1yd) green noil silk 114cm (45in) wide

❖

1.1m (1¼ yd) cotton domette

❖

80cm (1yd) backing fabric 114cm (45in) wide

❖

1 reel of yellow buttonhole thread

❖

2 reels of yellow cotton thread

❖

Dressmaker's 5cm (2in) graphpaper

❖

Dressmaker's carbon and serrated wheel

❖

Masking tape

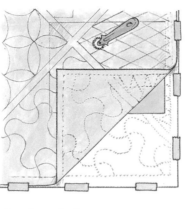

1 *Enlarge the design onto dressmaker's graphpaper to measure 99 x 69cm (39 x 27in) as shown on page 97. Cut the silk, domette and backing fabric 110 x 80cm (43 x 32in). Tape the domette to a table, centre the design over the domette and hold in place with masking tape. Slip a sheet of dressmaker's carbon between the design and the domette with the carbon side down and, using the serrated wheel, draw over the design. Small dots will appear on the domette.*

Speedy Sashiko

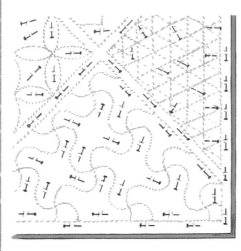

2 *Using either straight or safety pins, pintack the silk and domette together, with the design showing on the back. All the designs are sewn from the wrong side of the quilt.*

3 *Fill the bobbin with buttonhole thread and loosen off the lower tension on the machine. Use normal sewing thread on the top of the machine and lengthen the stitch slightly. Practise on a spare piece of fabric. Stitch the centre design, following the order of stitching shown on the template opposite on page 75 in order to cut down on the number of ends to be tied off.*

4 *Next work the zig-zag designs on either side of the centre motif. When the line of stitching changes direction, leave the needle in the work, lift the presser foot and pivot, lower the presser foot and continue (see page 107). Pull the ends through to the back and knot. Continue working all the different designs in the same way.*

5 *Change the bobbin to normal sewing thread, tighten up the lower tension and shorten the stitch length to about 2.5 (2¹/₂). Machine stitch over the lines which surround the stitch designs. These lines will be your guide for the satin stitch details, which are worked from the right side.*

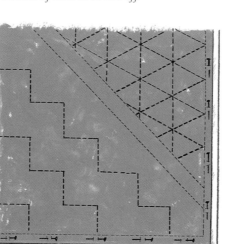

6 *Trim the edges of the quilt to 1cm (¹/₂in) from the machine line, and the domette slightly narrower. Wrap the edges of the quilt top towards the back, enclosing the domette, and pin. Place over the backing fabric.*

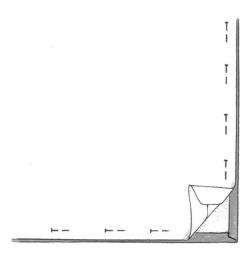

7 *Turn in the edges of the backing fabric, so that it is slightly smaller than the quilt top, and pin in place.*

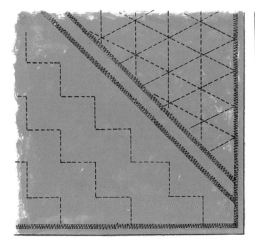

8 *To finish, work a wide satin stitch over all the straight stitch guide lines. The satin stitch worked at the edges will secure the hem.*

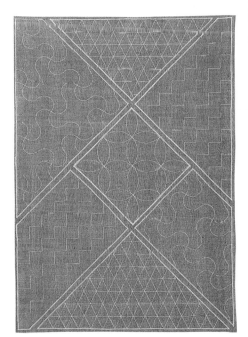

SPEEDY SASHIKO CHARTED TEMPLATE:
1 SQ = 5CM (2IN)

Threadlines

The luscious gleam of dupion silk perfectly complements creative but simple quilting stitches. The design is inspired by patchwork, each shape filled with machined straight stitch worked backwards and forwards until each section is filled. Only four colours are used, red, yellow, blue and green, but blended with cream thread they produce a surprising variety of tones. The finished size of the quilt is 78cm (31in) square.

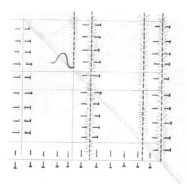

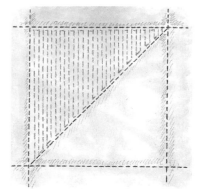

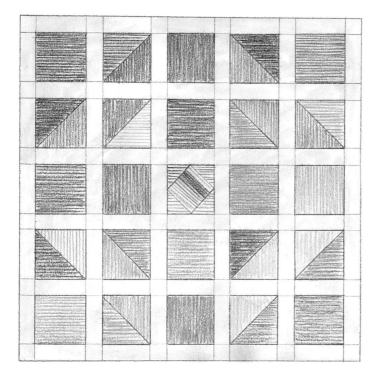

2 Cut the silk and the wadding into 1m (1yd) squares. Lay the silk right side down on a table and hold the edges in place with masking tape. Layer the wadding and the backing with the drawn design, right side up. Pin horizontally on the drawn lines. Remove the masking tape and machine stitch over all the drawn lines of the design, using cream thread and the walking foot (see page 106).

3 Straight stitch is used to fill in the shapes according to the design shown in step 1. Sew a line using stitch size 2.5, ending with the needle remaining in the fabric at the last stitch. Gently roll the handwheel towards you to lift the foot and shift the work a stitch length sideways. Press the reverse needle and sew back to where you started. Continue to fill in the squares and triangles in this way, working to the colour scheme shown. Use a mixture of coloured and cream threads to achieve paler colours. Keep the thread ends trimmed.

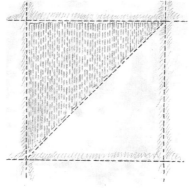

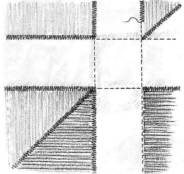

WORKBASKET

❖

1m (1yd) cream dupion silk 114cm (45in) wide

❖

1m (1yd) square needlepunch wadding

❖

1m (1yd) backing fabric 114cm (45in) wide

❖

2 reels each of size 30 glossy rayon machine embroidery thread in red, yellow, blue and green

❖

6 reels, size 30, of cream glossy rayon machine embroidery thread

❖

Sharp soft lead or quilter's pencil

1 Either make several photocopies, or trace out the design above to use as a template for working out the colour combinations using red, yellow, green and blue thread. Cut the backing fabric into an accurate metre (yard) square and rule or press diagonal folds from the corners. Using these lines as corner guides, measure and draw with a sharp pencil an accurate square of 73cm (28in). Following the chart, draw the border and sashing lines onto the backing fabric.

4 In order not to be continually changing thread, work the squares and triangles, using one colour after the other. Then start stitching with a second colour and begin mixing with the previous stitched lines. Take care to stop stitching when the grid lines are reached.

5 When all the shapes are filled, work one or two lines of satin stitch across the diagonal lines. Some machines have a sloping satin stitch, so three lines may be worked. Using cream thread, work satin stitch around the squares, knotting thread ends on the back (see page 106).

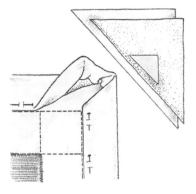

6 *The close stitching will have distorted the edges of the quilt, so utilize this fullness by making a puffed border. Pin the silk and the wadding out of the way, and trim the backing to 1.5cm (¹/₂in) from the outside sewn guideline on all four sides using the rotary cutter. Trim the wadding to 8cm (3¹/₄in). Trim the corner triangles away from the quilt top, wadding and backing, so that a mitred fold can be made (see page 105).*

Cut a hanging sleeve for the quilt 72 x 9cm (28¹/₂ x 3¹/₂in). Sew a hem on the short edges, and press a fold along one long edge. Make a double fold in the wadding and silk, pin and slip stitch close to the sewn guideline, incorporating the hanging sleeve (see page 107). If the quilt hangs with wobbly edges, sew an invisible running stitch inside the stitched guideline and gently pull into a square shape.

If you want to get some confidence in this kind of machine embroidery first, practise on an offcut of silk, wadding and backing before you start.

Cherubs

Cherubs holding swags welcome a new baby on this charming cot quilt. It features free-machine meander quilting, which gives an interesting texture and throws into relief the swags, bows, cherubs, stars and heart motifs. If you are new to free-machine sewing, try quilting the area between the heart and swags and leaving the remaining areas unquilted. We used a slightly darker yellow thread to emphasize the stitching. The finished quilt size is 100 x 70cm (40 x 28in).

WORKBASKET
✤

1.7m (2yd) yellow cotton fabric 114cm (45in) wide

✤

110 X 80cm (44 X 32in) wadding

✤

1 reel of thread slightly darker than the yellow fabric

✤

Dressmaker's 5cm (2in) graphpaper

✤

Waterproof felt-tipped pen

✤

Sharp quilter's pencil

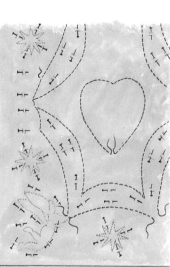

1 *Cut two binding strips 4cm (1¹/2in) wide from the top of the yellow fabric, and cut one from the side. Cut the remainder of the fabric into two equal pieces. Enlarge in full the half design opposite onto 5cm (2in) dressmaker's graphpaper (see page 97). Tape the design to the table (a white background helps) and tape one piece of the yellow fabric over the top. Using a quilter's pencil, trace the design onto the fabric. Add the child's name.*

2 *Pin tack the top, wadding and backing together (see page 104) and prepare to free-machine sew (see page 106). Working from the centre, sew along the lines, first of the heart and then the swags and bows and lastly the cherubs. Plan the stitching lines so that you do not have to stop and start too often. When the motifs are finished, pull the threads through to the back and knot (see page 106). Work the name of the child with free-machine straight stitch.*

Starting from the centre, sew the meander quilting (see page 106) in small areas, working slowly and manipulating the fabric so that squiggles appear rather like pieces of a jigsaw. Take a rest from time to time as this is close work.

When all the stitching is finished, trim the edges straight with a rotary cutter (see page 102) and attach the bindings (see pages 104–105).

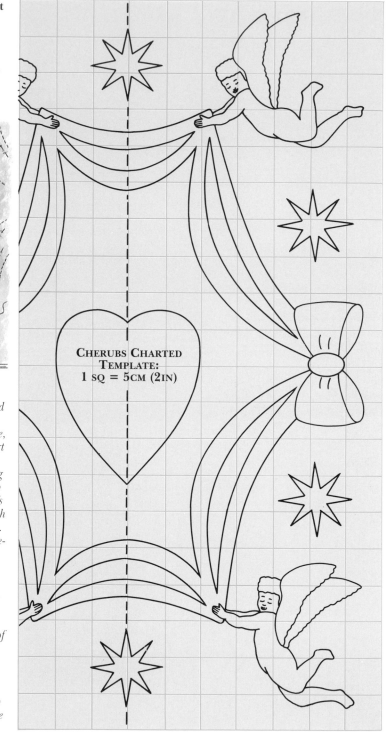

CHERUBS CHARTED TEMPLATE:
1 SQ = 5CM (2IN)

Bedtime with the Animals

By choosing one striking fabric with interesting motifs you can achieve really exciting effects. This single bed quilt, suitable for a child, was made simply by free machining around the various animals and fish within the design. Any cotton fabric with a large enough motif can be turned into a wonderful bed cover in this way. Only one length of lightweight furnishing fabric, which comes wide enough to cover the bed, is needed so no piecing is required. To complete it add a generous binding. The finished size is 239 x 150cm (94 x 59in).

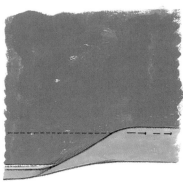

WORKBASKET
❖

2.5m (2³/4yd) light furnishing fabric with large motifs 148cm (58in) wide
❖

2.5m (2³/4yd) cotton backing fabric 152cm (60in) wide
❖

80cm (³/4yd) contrasting cotton fabric 114cm (45in) wide
❖

243 X 152cm (96 x 60in) wadding
❖

4 reels toning thread for machine quilting

1 *Lay the backing fabric on the floor or on a table right side down and tape in place. Lay the wadding over on top and trim away any excess. Place the quilt fabric on top and pin tack (see page 105).*

Work out which motifs you wish to feature, planning how you can stitch from one to another without having to start a new line of machining. This will cut down on the threads which have to be pulled through to the wrong side, knotted and sewn in. Follow the instructions for free-machine stitching given on page 106 to sew around the motifs. When you have sufficient stitching to hold the wadding, knot and sew in any ends from the back (see page 106).

2 *If the edges of the quilt have distorted, straighten as shown on page 102. Cut five strips of binding 11.5cm (4¹/2in) wide and join to make one long length. Sew the binding onto the sides first (see "Folding towards the back", pages 104–105), then the top and bottom, setting it in 3cm (1¹/2in) from the edge. This will make a wide binding.*

3 *Fold the binding to the back, turn in a small hem and stitch either by hand or machine. If machining on a binding, pin on the right side, checking that the folded edge at the back is directly under the seam formed when the binding was attached. Machine from the right side "in the ditch" (see page 106) of the binding seam, so that the new stitching line is not visible on top, but sews down the hem underneath.*

New Views

The four exuberant quilts seen here have been designed for speed in construction, use of colour and tone and their visual impact. Enjoy collecting and using unusual fabrics to make quilts with a modern twist.

Deco Delight

At first, it is not easy to see whether this quilt is a curved or diagonal block. It is in fact both, and much simpler than it appears. This project is more suitable for the experienced patchworker. The finished size is 218 x 187cm (86 x 74in).

WORKBASKET

✤

50cm (½yd) each of light and medium yellow cotton fabric 114cm (45in) wide

✤

50cm (½yd) each of light and medium lime green cotton fabric 114cm (45in) wide

✤

1.1m (1¼yd) each of light and medium apricot cotton fabric 114cm (45in) wide

✤

1m (1yd) each of light and medium turquoise cotton fabric 114cm (45in) wide

✤

30cm (⅓yd) each of light and medium lavender cotton fabric 114cm (45in) wide

✤

2.3m (2½yd) darker turquoise cotton fabric 114cm (45in) wide

✤

5m (5yd) cotton backing fabric 114cm (45in) wide, joined to make a piece the same size as the top

✤

228 x 197cm (90 x 78in) wadding

✤

3 reels cream cotton thread for piecing

✤

1 reel clear nylon monofilament thread for quilting

✤

Dressmaker's 5cm (2in) graphpaper

✤

Template plastic 30cm (12in) square

✤

Waterproof pen

✤

Double-sided sticky tape

1 *Enlarge the block on page 86 to 30cm (12in) by transferring the design onto 5cm (2in) graphpaper (see page 97). Trace the design onto template plastic, using a waterproof pen. Mark all the template numbers, grainlines, balance marks (the tiny double lines), and the arrows on either side of the diagonal join. All these marks will help to prevent mistakes. Numbers and balance marks on one side of the diagonal line are even, on the other side, odd.*

Put a stationery dot onto each template to identify the right side. Put small pieces of double-sided sticky tape onto the back of each template, then carefully cut out the block.

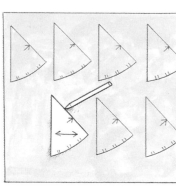

2 *Note that the block is shown in reverse. Place the templates on the wrong side of the fabric and draw around – this will ensure that the block makes up with the diagonal in the same direction as the illustrated quilt. Peel the backing from the sticky tape and place template 9 right side up on the wrong side of the pale yellow fabric, keeping the grainline straight. Draw around the template with a fine lead pencil 15 times, marking balance marks and arrows and leaving a seam allowance of approximately 7.5mm (¼in) around each piece. Repeat for template 10. Next draw around templates 9 and 10 on the medium yellow fabric in the same way.*

Continue drawing around all the templates on the appropriate fabrics until 15 have been cut from each template in each colour. Draw around templates 7 and 8 for the light and medium lime green fabrics, 5 and 6 for the light and medium apricot fabrics, 3 and 4 for the light and medium turquoise fabrics and 1 and 2 for the light and medium lavender fabrics.

3 *Sort out all the cut pieces into piles so that you can work efficiently and quickly. Tacking curved seams before machine sewing will take longer, but careful pinning will save time. Prepare the pieces to be sewn, pinning together in pairs, and matching medium to medium and light to light colours, pieces number 8 and 10, 7 and 9, 4 and 6, 3 and 5. First pin into each end, putting the pin through the corner and the sides of the drawn line. This will keep the edges straight. Next, push a pin through the matching balance marks, pinning on the drawn lines, as shown, making sure they are correctly aligned. Continue adding pins between the balance marks. Machine sew over the pins, then check for accuracy. It is wise to make any corrections at this stage – often just a few stitches need to be realigned. Sew a few trial pieces before going onto the next step.*

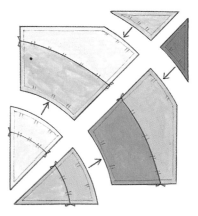

4 *Continue by joining piece numbers 7 to 5 and 8 to 6 in the same way, finally adding 1 to 3 and 2 to 4.*

Deco Delight

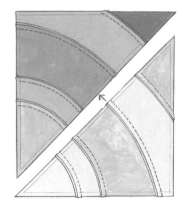

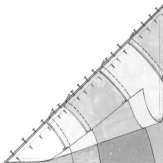

6 (*Right*). *Next pair up a medium and a light triangle to make a square with the curves matching. As the fabric is on the bias, use plenty of pins. Machine chain fashion (see page 100), checking for accuracy. Press, opening the seams flat (see page 100). There should now be 15 blocks with the darker fabric on the top left (A) and 15 with the darker fabric bottom left (B). Make two separate piles of these blocks.*

DECO DELIGHT CHARTED
TEMPLATE: 1 SQ = 2.5CM (1IN)

5 (*Above*). *Trim neatly to 7.5mm (¹/4in), then press the curved seam allowances on the pale-coloured triangles towards the yellow fabric and on the medium-coloured triangles towards the lilac. This will help the seams to sit well.*

There are now four different versions of the triangle. Sort them into two piles of medium and light. Sort both piles into two further piles, according to the direction of the curves.

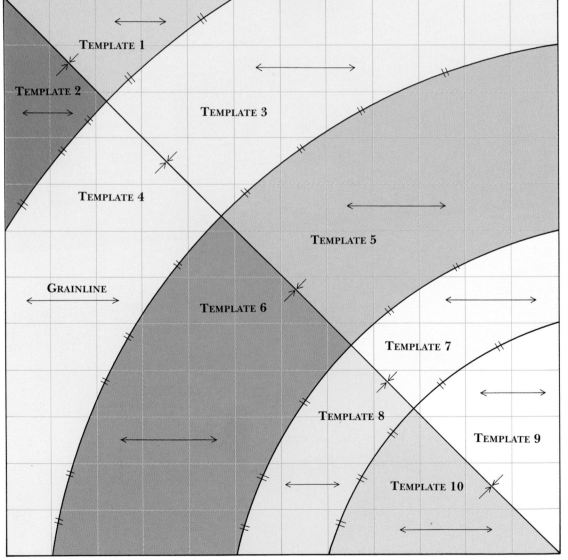

TEMPLATE 1

TEMPLATE 2

TEMPLATE 3

TEMPLATE 4

TEMPLATE 5

GRAINLINE

TEMPLATE 6

TEMPLATE 7

TEMPLATE 8

TEMPLATE 9

TEMPLATE 10

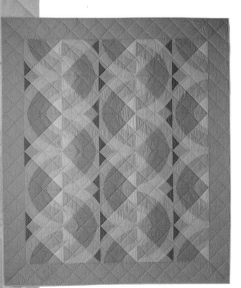

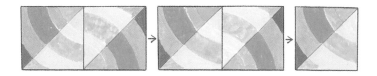

7 *Study the diagram to see how the blocks are arranged for the first row. The top row, using block A, starts at the left with the darker side of the triangle in the top corner. Twist the next block A 180 degrees, so that the lime green curves meet. Repeat with five more pairs of A blocks. Pin together and chain sew. Pin together these pairs in three sets of four blocks, keeping each pair the same way up. Study the diagram for accuracy. Finally add a fifth block, the same way up as before, to the right end of each row to make three rows of A blocks.*

8 *For the alternate row, and starting from the left, place block B with the darker side bottom left and turn the next block B so that the lime green curves meet. Repeat with five more pairs of B blocks. Pin together in pairs and chain sew as before, finally adding the single block to three rows of B blocks. Trim the seam allowances slightly and then press the seams open.*

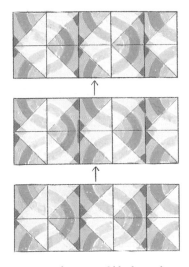

9 *Lay out the rows of blocks and then pin and sew in pairs, checking that the joins match. Trim the seam allowances slightly and press open.*

Cut the turquoise fabric into borders 20cm (8in) wide, two 220cm (88in) and two 190cm (76in) long. Attach to the pieced quilt top with mitred corners as shown on pages 102–103. Press well.

10 *Mark diagonal lines 10cm (4in) apart, using a quilting ruler and a thin sliver of soap or a light pencil.*

Sandwich the top, wadding and backing together as shown on page 104, then pin tack on the lines in the direction of sewing (see page 105), so that the pins can be slid out as the machine needle approaches.

The quilting is worked using clear monofilament nylon on the top and white cotton on the bobbin. To avoid any problems using nylon thread, loosen both the top and the bobbin tension by only half a turn. Test, adjusting both tensions gradually until there is a perfect stitch top and bottom. This will prevent any damage to the machine. Be sure to return the tensions to their original setting before the next step.

Machine quilt along the marked diagonal lines (see page 106). Straighten the edges and measure before cutting and joining a narrow binding 5cm (2in) wide. Bind according to the instructions on pages 104–105.

Safari Adventure

This wall quilt uses a striped fabric, pieced in several different ways, to give the effect of an exotic rug. Striped fabrics enable you to take shortcuts with designs which would normally need pieced strips. The multi-coloured fabric used here has an uneven painted effect which has the advantage of not needing precise matching. The fabric you choose will probably have different width strips from ours, or you could even paint your own as shown on page 46. This is a project for the more advanced quilter. The finished size is 120 x 84cm (47 x 33in).

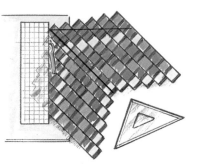

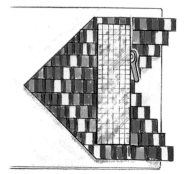

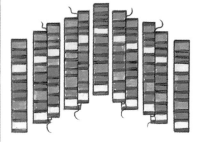

WORKBASKET

❖

2m (2yd) multi-coloured striped cotton fabric 114cm (45in) wide with the stripes running width ways

❖

50cm (1/2yd) contrasting orange speckled cotton fabric 114cm (45in) wide

❖

40cm (1/2yd) each of plain terracotta and rust cotton fabric 114cm (45in) wide

❖

130 x 114cm (48 x 45in) cotton backing fabric

❖

150 x 90cm (60 x 36in) needlepunch wadding

❖

1 reel each of threads in black, terracotta, lime green and purple for piecing and machine quilting

❖

Card

❖

Pencil

1 *Cut a piece of the striped material 30cm (12in) long across the width, using a rotary cutter and ruler (see page 99). Cut down, across the strips, 22 5cm (2in) strips.*

Take one strip and decide on the dominant colour stripe. Lay a second strip beside the first and drop the dominant colour stripe so that its top edge is set one step below its partner on strip one. Continue both sides of the first strip, until a V-shaped pattern can be seen. Pin horizontally (see page 100) in pairs and machine chain fashion (see page 100). Chain piece the pairs together according to your layout. Then join to the single centre and side strips, joining all pieces. Repeat with the remaining 11 strips. Press the seams to one side (see page 100).

2 *Mark the centre of the middle strip and use a set square or bias rule to cut a 45 degree angle on each side of both pieces.*

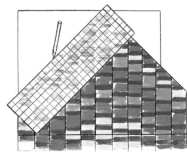

4 *Make a triangle template to fit the corners by squaring off the diamond on a piece of card. Cut eight triangles from the contrast fabric, with a seam allowance on all sides. Sew four to the corners of the diamond. Press.*

3 *Cut a straight line along the bottom edge of each triangle level with the bottom of the centre strip. Sew the two together, right sides facing, along the bottom edge. The pattern will form a diamond. Press the seam open.*

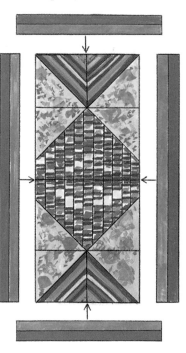

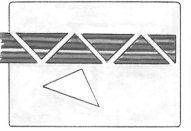

5 *Cut another strip across the width of the fabric, cutting along the direction of the stripes, and deep enough to fit the triangle used in step 3. Place the template on the strip and cut four triangles as illustrated above, adding seam allowances on all three sides.*

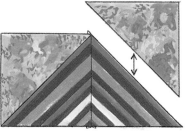

6 *Join two striped triangles together so that a chevron forms in the centre. Add a contrast triangle either side. Repeat for the remaining triangles. Join these two pieces at either end of the main piece, matching the point of the chevron with that of the diamond.*

7 *Using two toning solid fabrics, cut four strips from each colour 5cm (2in) wide to fit each side. Sew together to make 8.5cm (3½in) widths and press before attaching to the sides. Repeat for the strips that are to fit along the top and bottom of the quilt top.*

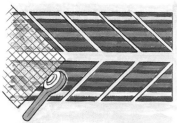

8 *Measure and cut two strips 5.5cm (6in) deep across the width of the striped fabric. Using a bias square, cut 18 10cm (4in) diagonal strips from left to right from one strip and 18 from right to left from the other. Join one strip from each side, so that a chevron pattern emerges. Pin in pairs and chain sew until you have two long strips of 18 each.*

9 *Cut off the triangle sides as shown to leave a strip approximately 15 cm (6in) wide. Measure to fit a strip on either side of the patchwork. Pin, right sides together, and sew. Measure and cut a 5cm (2in) strip to fit across the width of the piece and sew on at the top and the bottom as before. Press well.*

Cut the wadding and backing (see page 104), then pin tack before machine quilting as shown on page 106. Quilt, following the stripes. Finish by cutting five strips 4cm (1¹/₂in) wide and bind, folding butt corners (see pages 104–105).

Bow Ties

Here is a quilt to bring a smile to your face. Made entirely from recycled ties and shirts, even the buttons have been utilized. Friends will join in the fun and help you to collect 64 ties. Select colours in tones of yellow, red, pink, blue, turquoise and green, with similar pale-coloured shirts. The easy construction leaves the knot of the tie slightly puffed. The shirt areas are machine meander quilted, with the machine moving through the corners from one square to another without stopping. Do try piecing a block before starting, the technique takes longer to explain than to make! The finished size of the quilt is 160.5cm (59in) square.

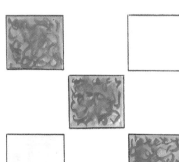

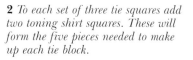

2 *To each set of three tie squares add two toning shirt squares. These will form the five pieces needed to make up each tie block.*

WORKBASKET
❖
64 ties of a similar weight washed but not unpicked. Use a mild detergent and gentle low heat programme in the washing machine
❖
4m (4yd) ultrasoft light interfacing
❖
A variety of shirt fabrics or similar weight cotton fabric
❖
70cm (³/4yd) dark blue border fabric
❖
1.6m (1³/4yd) wadding
❖
1.7m (1³/4yd) cotton backing fabric 152cm (70in) wide
❖
1 reel each of black cotton thread and thread to tone for piecing
❖
2 reels clear nylon monofilament thread for quilting
❖
60 shirt buttons

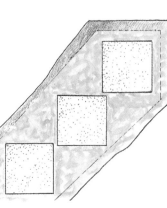

1 *Using a rotary cutter and (see page 99) cut 196 squares 9.5cm (3¹/2in) and 64 strips 28.5 x 9.5cm (10¹/2 x 3¹/2in) from the interfacing. These will be used as backing for the ties, stabilizing and preventing the ties from fraying as well as avoiding showthrough on the shirt fabrics. Unpick the ties and press (see pages 100–101).*

Iron three squares of interfacing onto the wrong side of each tie. Make sure the straight edges run along the grain of the material. Iron the strips of interfacing onto the wrong side of the shirts. Using the rotary cutter and ruler cut out three squares from each tie (do not rely on the interfacing for an exact square, it often distorts during pressing) and three 9.5cm (3¹/2in) squares from the strips of interfacing-backed shirting.

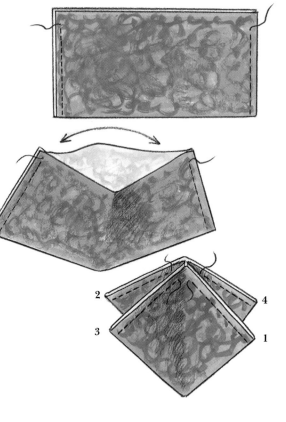

3 *Fold the centre square of each block in half horizontally and sew both sides with a narrow seam allowance just under 7.5mm (¹/4in), starting 7.5mm (¹/4in) from the top. Push the open top corners together and sew down the resulting two*

sides, leaving 7.5mm (¹/4in) space at the top as before. The pocket forms the knot of the bow tie. Prepare and sew each step chain method (see page 100) for speed and efficiency, being sure to leave the top 7.5mm (¹/4in) unsewn.

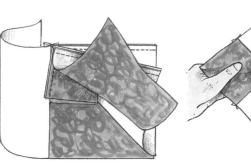

4 *Sandwich seam 1 of the pocket between one tie piece and one shirt piece right sides together. Again leave 7.5mm (¹/₄in) at the beginning of the seam and stitch together, taking a seam allowance of 7.5mm (¹/₄in).*

5 *Refold the pocket and sandwich seam 2 between the unsewn right angle of the tie square from step 4 and the second shirt square. Sew and refold. Add the final tie square and sandwich seam 3 between the previously sewn shirt and the final square of fabric.*

6 *Lastly sandwich seam 4 and pull open the four corners – a bow tie will appear before you!*

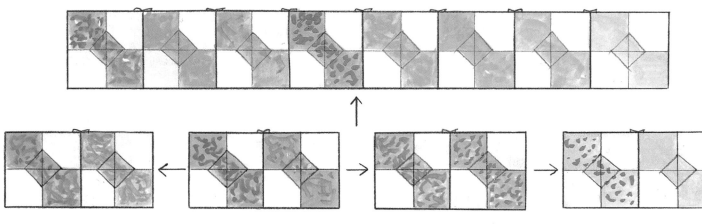

7 *Arrange the blocks in eight rows of eight, so that the colours "wash" diagonally across the quilt top, The quilt shown here starts with the yellow tones at the top left hand corner and, working diagonally, moves towards orange red, pink, blue, and turquoise with green in*

the bottom right hand corner. The effect you achieve will depend on the range of colours in the ties selected. Sew together, first in pairs, chain method, then in lengths, before joining the lengths together to make a square.

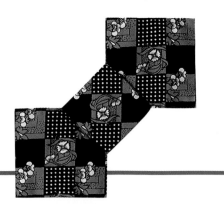

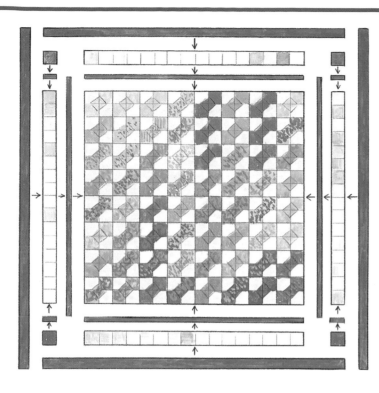

To make up the quilt, sandwich the quilt top, wadding and backing (see page 104). Following instructions for free-machine quilting (see page 106), meander quilt on the shirts, wandering from one square to another without stopping sewing. When the quilting is finished, sew buttons around the border in the centre of the shirt squares. Finally, cut four binding strips 161 x 3cm (60 x 1¹/2in) and, following the instructions on page 104–105, attach to the quilt. Fold the binding to the back and slip stitch.

8 To make the borders, check the length and width of the quilt, which should now be 129.5cm (48¹/2in) square. Machine stitch the remaining shirt squares into four strips of 16 squares each.

Using the rotary cutter, cut eight strips from the navy blue fabric 4cm (1¹/2in) wide, two 129.5cm (48¹/2in) long, two 150.5cm (50¹/2in) long and four 9.5cm (3¹/2in) long. Cut four strips 6.5cm (2¹/2in) wide, two 150.5cm (50¹/2in) long and two 160.5cm (59in) long. Cut out four 9.5cm (3¹/2in) squares from ties for the corners, using the remaining interfacing squares.

Join the two 129.5 x 4cm (48¹/2 x 1¹/2in) narrow blue border strips to two of the shirting border strips. Stitch these to the sides of the quilt, with the blue strip innermost, and lining up the squares in the border with those in the quilt.

Add one 9.5 x 4cm (3¹/2 x 1¹/2in) strip to each end of the two remaining shirting borders. Next add one 9.5cm (3¹/2in) tie square to each end of these two border strips. Join each of these border strips to a 150.5 x 4cm (50¹/2 x 2¹/2) blue strip. Attach to the top and bottom of the quilt, blue strip innermost.

Stitch the two 150.5 x 6.5cm (50¹/2 x 2¹/2in) strips to the sides of the quilt and the two remaining strips to the top and bottom of the quilt.

Bojangles

Named after a famous American tap dancer of the 1930s, the black and white fabrics on this quilt have a rhythm all of their own. Although the quilt design appears complex, it uses simple and quick strip piecing techniques. The fabrics are graded and appear darker or lighter according to the proportions of white/black, giving the effect of movement, whilst the 16 piece blocks of colour provide contrast. We used eight solid colours, but four would work perfectly well. To get a good selection of black and white patterns, look for both dress and craft fabrics. Read the instructions on page 100 carefully, these explain how to press seam allowances so that perfect joins can be achieved. The finished quilt measures 230 x 130cm (92 x 56in) and would be perfect for a dance or music lover.

WORKBASKET
❖

16 strips 114 x 6.5cm
(45 x 2¹/₂in) cut from cotton
fabric in eight solid colours in
2 tones of 4 colours

❖

30cm (¹/₃yd) cotton fabric
114cm (45in) wide showing
white stars on black

❖

30cm (¹/₃yd) black and white
wavy striped cotton fabric
114cm (45in) wide

❖

25cm (¹/₄yd) each of three cotton
fabrics 114cm (45in) wide
showing black designs on white

❖

25cm (¹/₄yd) each of seven black
and white cotton fabrics 114cm
(45in) wide, toning dark to light

❖

2.5m (2²/₃yd) black border cotton
fabric 114cm (45in) wide

❖

2.5m (2²/₃yd) backing cotton
fabric 152cm (60in) wide

❖

250 x 152cm (96 x 60in)
medium-weight wadding

❖

Stranded embroidery threads in
various colours for knotting

❖

1 reel beige cotton thread for
piecing coloured fabric

❖

1 reel black cotton thread
for quilting

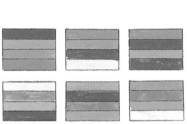

1 *To make the 16-patch coloured blocks, use the rotary cutter (see page 99) to cut a total of 24 strips 6.5cm (2¹/₂in) wide from the eight solid fabrics. Lay out the strips into six arrangements of four colours each. Pin and machine sew chain fashion (see page 100).*

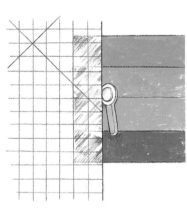

2 *Using the quilter's rule and board (see page 99), measure and cut eight strips 6.5cm (2¹/₂in) wide from each of the six colour combinations. This will make 48 strips. Lay out the strips to form blocks of 16 squares, so that the colours are well distributed and press the seam allowances of adjoining strips in opposite directions so that the joins will sit accurately (see page 100).*

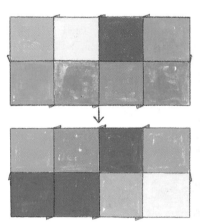

3 *Sew together in pairs, chain fashion, until 12 blocks have been sewn. Press well.*

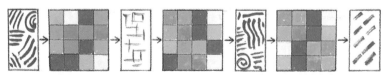

4 *From the black design on white fabrics, cut sixteen 21.5 x 11.5cm (8¹/₂ x 4¹/₂in) pieces. Arrange the designs and attach either side of the coloured blocks to make four strips.*

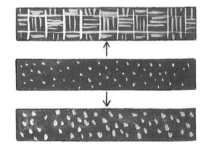

5 *Cut 16 pieces 16.5 x 11.5cm (6¹/₂ x 4¹/₂in) from the striped fabric. Select three fabric tones and cut three strips from each 6.5cm (2¹/₂in) wide. Join the three strips and press well.*

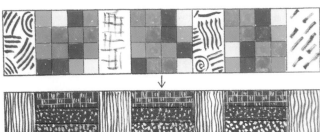

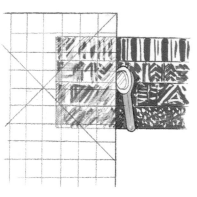

7 *Cut two strips 6.5cm (2¹/₂in) wide from each of the remaining four black and white fabrics and 16 pieces 16.5 x 11.5cm (6¹/₂ x 4¹/₂in) from the star fabric. Join the strips arranging them so that the tones run from dark to light. Press. Cut 12 16.5cm (6¹/₂in) strips.*

6 *Cut 12 21.5cm (8¹/₂in) pieces from the strips and join them to the striped fabric as shown in the diagram to make four strips. These strips can now be sewn to the coloured blocks strips.*

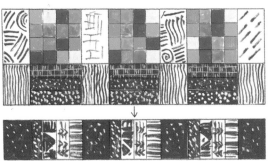

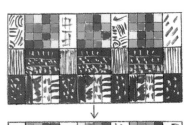

8 *Join them to the star pieces making four strips. Attach to the black and white strips as in the previous step. There should now be four wide strips measuring 51.5 x 101.5cm (20¹/₂ x 40¹/₂in).*

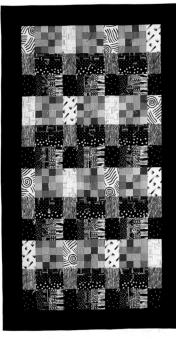

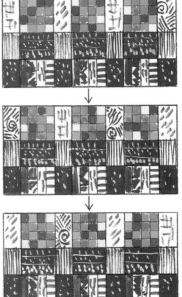

Decorative knots (see page 107) are used as quilting, a traditional and speedy technique. Work from the front, with stranded embroidery thread and an embroidery needle, which has a long eye, making threading much quicker. Distribute the knots evenly across the quilt, using long strands of thread. Tie a reef knot and trim the ends to leave about 2.5cm (1in).

Smooth out the quilt and pin horizontally (see page 100) across the seam where the main quilt meets the borders. Machine quilt in the ditch (see page 106).

Pin the three layers of the border to hold them smooth and straight and mark up two quilting lines, parallel to and approximately 5cm (2in) from the border seam and each other. Use a quilter's rule and soap, which shows up well on black. Machine quilt (see page 106) along these lines. If the walking foot has a guide bar, line it up with the the previous quilting sewn in the ditch, Trim the edges of the quilt, using a square quilter's rule, rotary cutter and board (see page 102).

Cut binding strips to fit and attach to the sides first, and finally the top and bottom (see pages 104–105). Slip stitch on the back.

9 *Join all the wide strips together and press well.*

From the black fabric, cut four borders 16.5cm (6¹/₂in) wide, two 201.5cm (80¹/₂in) long and two 132.5cm (52¹/₂in) long. Attach the borders, sides first, then top and bottom, as shown on pages 102–103. Sandwich the top, wadding and backing together, and pintack (see pages 104 and 105).

Techniques

In the following section you will learn the first steps in making the projects in this book as well as the final steps in finishing them off. The information is accessible, yet thorough so that beginners can start from basics, learning quickly and enjoyably. More experienced quilters will find new techniques to practise.

You will find sewing your quilt easier, and the final quilt more satisfactory, if you always use 100 per cent cotton fabrics unless otherwise specified. Remember that seam allowances of 7.5mm (^{1}/4in) are included in all cutting instructions unless otherwise specified.

MAKING A TEMPLATE

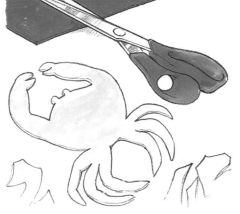

DRAWING AROUND A TEMPLATE

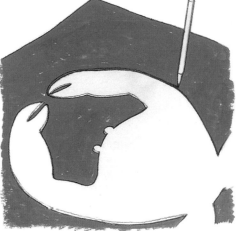

ENLARGING A DESIGN

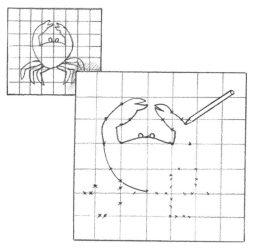

Make templates from card or special plastic which is easy to cut with scissors or a craftknife. They should be marked with the straight grainline and numbered using a waterproof pen. Place a piece of double-sided sticky tape on the wrong side to hold the template in place on the fabric. Never leave sticky tape on fabric overnight as the glue will leave a mark which is impossible to remove. It is also a good idea to name the pieces, so that they can be filed away in plastic bags until needed again.

A small, coloured sticky label (sold by stationers, in various sizes and colours) is a useful device to recognize quickly which side of a template should be used.

Always use a very fine pencil point to draw around templates to minimize distortion. Hold the pencil point vertically, close to the template edge and try not to drag the fabric. A special quilter's pencil with washable lead is excellent on paler fabrics and a silver pencil shows up on dark colours. Sheets of fine glasspaper from DIY shops, glued to a piece of cardboard stops fabrics (including silk) from shifting and helps to give a fine line.

Project designs can be quickly enlarged by hand. Draw a square or rectangle to the size of the finished design onto a sheet of paper. Divide up with a series of vertical and horizontal lines, starting from the centre outwards, drawn approximately 8cm (3in) apart. Draw the same number of lines on a piece of tracing paper taped over the design in the book. Examine how the lines fall in each square on the small design and repeat on the full size pattern. Transfer all grain, balance marks and template numbers onto the full sized drawing. The original is now the key drawing to be used as a reference. Dressmaker's pattern paper comes in useful sizes, but a trip to a local printer may also yield large sheets of paper.

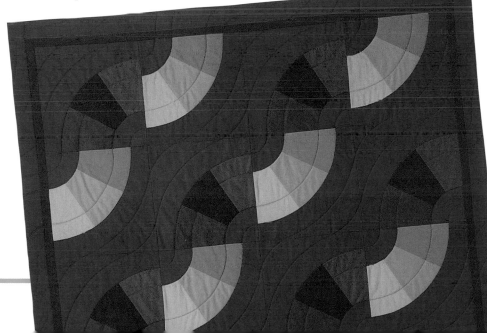

Techniques

STITCHES

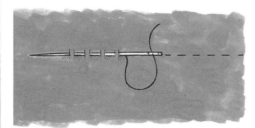

Running stitch The running stitch is worked from right to left, starting with a knot or double stitch. Use a Sharp needle, and load it with two or three stitches, keeping them the same size, before pulling through.

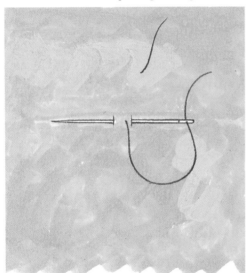

Quilting Stitch The quilting stitch is a small version of a running stitch sewn using a Between needle. A strong, specially coated thread is needed either in cotton or cotton covered polyester. Uncoated threads need to be pulled through a block of beeswax to give them strength and help them pass easily through the fabric.

1 Cut a length of quilting thread about 40cm (16in) and tie a knot in one end. Insert the needle about 2.5cm (1in) away from the quilting line and give a little tug to pull the knot into the wadding. Make a

small back stitch then sew even single stitches or load the needle, whichever feels more comfortable. Make sure that the needle passes through all three layers with a neat stitch showing on the back. Check from time to time that the thread is not wearing in the needle eye, which would weaken the quilting.

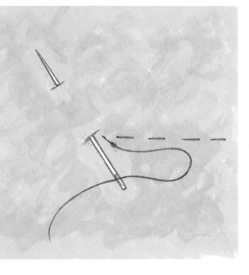

2 About 8cm (3in) from the end of the thread, make a knot and gently slide it close to the work using the point of the needle. Give a tug so that it disappears into the quilt top, work a double stitch and lose the end of the thread in the wadding, carefully trimming about 5cm (2in) from the knot.

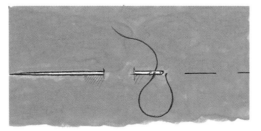

Tacking or basting stitch Tacking or basting requires large running stitches, usually worked with a long needle called a Straw. Tacking thread is an unpolished cotton thread, rather hairy so that it holds the quilt layers in place. It snaps easily, so will not break quilting stitches or tear the fabric as it is pulled out.

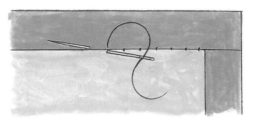

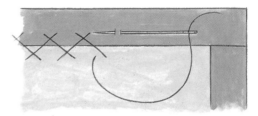

Slip stitch Slip stitch should only show a tiny dot of thread. It is worked from right to left, through the fold of the fabric to be attached. Make sure that the needle exits and enters one point above the other, rather than travelling on the surface of the fabric which will make a slanting stitch. Use the inside of the quilt, or folded fabric to move the needle along.

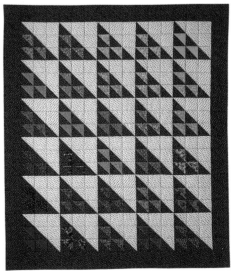

Herringbone stich Herringbone stitch is worked from the left, each stitch sewn towards the left, then crossing over and moving towards the right and above or below for the next stitch.

ROTARY CUTTING

There are some basic rules to keep in mind to ensure safe and successful rotary cutting. Always stand with your body facing, straight on, in the direction you will be cutting, which should be away from your body. The rotary blade is very sharp and the shield should be closed after every cut. Clear plenty of space around the cutting area, so that mishaps do not happen to surrounding fabrics. Take care there are no pins hiding under fabric to be cut. Only use the cutter on special self-healing boards which do not blunt the blade.

Before starting to cut out, take a little time to list how many components each block requires. Either stick a snip of the appropriate fabric alongside each template number or attach pieces to the block design. This will help prevent muddles.

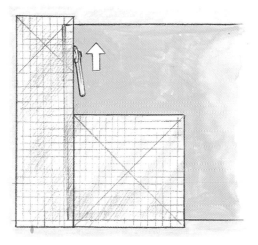

Straightening the fabric edge It is important to work with the grain straight on the fabric. Start by straightening one edge of the fabric either by cutting along the grain or pulling a thread right the way across from selvedge to selvedge. Cut off the selvedge edges. These are very tightly woven and tend to shrink up, distorting the main grain and gathering the edges. Pull the fabric, when it is slightly damp, across the bias, until the cut edge and selvedges are at right angles. A second pair of hands is helpful here. Fold the fabric in half or quarters and place the long and square rule as shown, to establish the fabric is straight.

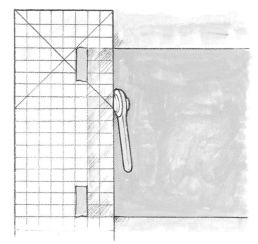

Cutting strips The measurements for rotary cutting given in the projects include seam allowances of 7.5mm (1/4in). Stick a piece of masking tape to the left of the relevant measurement ruler (right if you are left handed) as a guide when there are a lot of strips of the same size to be cut.

Before cutting, line up the folded edge of the fabric against a horizontal gridline on the board and the cut edge with a vertical line. This will ensure that the strips will be straight and not have a kink where the fold falls. Right-handed people should always have the fabric to the right and the ruler to the left, left-handed people should work vice versa. Cover the fabric with the ruler, aligning the relevant measurement guide with the trimmed edge of the fabric. Apply pressure to stop the ruler from moving. Spread your fingers across the ruler with your little finger off the left hand side, stopping the ruler from slipping. Keep your hand away from the cutting edge.

Cut with the edge of the blade against the ruler and using a firm pressure. It is kinder to hands and shoulders to run the blade across the fabric twice with a firm pressure, rather than pressing down hard. When making long strips, gently slide your fingers along to the end of the ruler when the blade has passed it. Take care not to disturb the layers. Check from time to time that the strips are still straight.

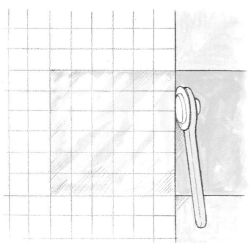

Cutting squares Stack between two to four layers of strips, matching the edges. Align the bottom edge of the strips with a horizontal guide on the mat or ruler and the left (right) edge with the measurement on the ruler. Cut across the strips with the rotary cutter to make squares.

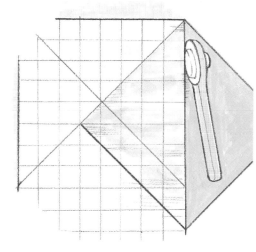

Cutting triangles Line up the edges of the fabric squares with the grid on the cutting mat as shown. Align using the right angle guide on the ruler with one edge of the square or a right angle edge of the triangle. If possible work on the corner of a table, so that you can walk round to make the second cut. If this is not possible, turn the whole mat around, not the fabric.

Techniques

PINNING

Whether to pin horizontally or vertically is largely a matter of personal choice. However, when sewing curved patchwork, horizontal pinning works well.

1 Vertically inserted pins are gently pulled out just as the machine needle reaches the point.

2 Horizontal pins can be machined over. Horizontal pinning blunts and breaks needles from time to time, which can be a slight disadvantage.

CHAIN PIECING

By laying out all the various components to be sewn, then pinning, much time and thread can be saved. With practice, pins need not be used, but be prepared to unpick! Lay out in two separate stacks the pieces that are to be joined. Make your chain piecing even faster by turning each stacked piece the same way and placing the two piles, right side up, so that a left piece flipped over the right is in the right position to be sewn. Flip over and pick up the first pieces to be machined and as they disappear behind the foot, run the machine for a couple of stitches and feed in the second set of pieces. Continue until all the pieces are sewn, check for accuracy, snip the connecting threads, and press.

PRESSING

It is important to understand that pressing and ironing are not the same. Ironing can push fabric out of shape. Gentle pressing and manipulating can, on the other hand, persuade fabric to behave beautifully. Steam irons give good, quick results, although some quilters prefer a damp cloth. It is usual to press the seam allowance towards the darker fabric to avoid show through, although sometimes it is necessary to press the seams open. Finally, always press on the right side of the fabric.

Pressing seams to one side
1 Press the seam allowance up along the edge of the iron.

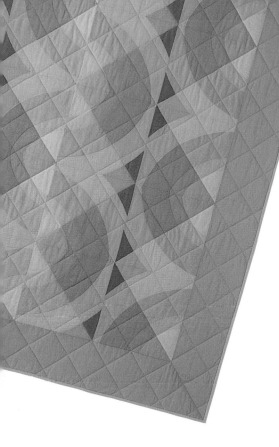

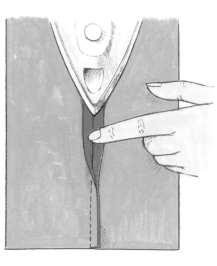

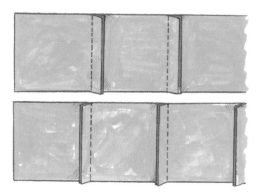

Pressing seams open Press seams open flat by running a finger along followed by the steam iron. The seams on quilt-as-you-go blocks are most efficiently pressed on the edge of the ironing board.

Setting in
1 By pressing the seam allowances in opposite directions, they will "sit in" making a perfect match.

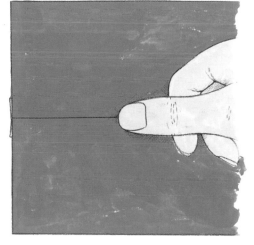

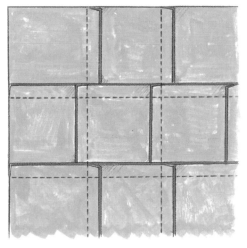

2 Lay the seam allowance to one side, making a crisp seam line.

Finger pressing Finger pressing is used in cases where the wadding might melt or flatten if touched by an iron. Run a thumb nail and clean finger along the seam.

2 When the strips have been joined, press the new seams all in the same direction.

Techniques

STRAIGHTENING EDGES

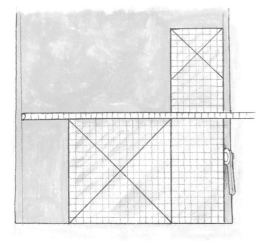

It is necessary to measure and check at intervals across and up the quilted piece before adding the final binding. The quilt will have shrunk a little, depending on the density, direction and the evenness of quilting distribution, so the sides will need to be straightened. Fold down the centre of the quilt and, using a tapemeasure, measure the narrowest width and mark a straight line with pencil or soap. Use a quilter's bias rule, set square and ruler to make guidemarks parallel to the edges of the quilt. Correct and mark the corners with the quilter's set square and ruler. Slide the self-healing mat under the quilt edge and trim with the rule and rotary cutter.

ATTACHING BORDERS

The decision as to whether to add a butt or mitred border depends on your experience and the design of the quilt top. If the design has very obvious diagonal lines then a mitre should be chosen. A butt border is easier to attach and uses slightly less fabric.

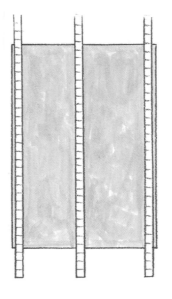

Measuring for borders Before cutting borders, measure the quilt on all sides and through the centre as shown. If there is no discrepancy, or if it is only slight, cut side borders from the centre measurements and ease the quilt top onto them. Measure for the top and bottom and cut border strips accordingly. Somehow, fabric has a mind of its own and the sides of the quilt top are often accidentally different sizes. If there is a great difference in the measurements, either examine the quilt top to see where this has occurred and correct, or make the borders longer. Measure down the centre of the quilt, cut both pairs of borders to match and ease or stretch them in.

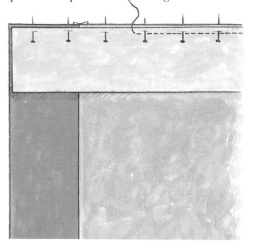

Butt border

1 It is more economical to measure and cut the side borders first (see left). After cutting out, fold the border lengths in half and quarters then mark with a pin or a finger pinch. Repeat on the quilt top. Pieced tops should be machined with the seam allowances laying the way they have been pressed, so by placing the border beneath on the machine, it is possible to check they have not moved while sewing. However, an overlong top is better sewn with the border positioned on top. Either way, match up marking pins and add plenty of horizontally positioned pins before sewing the seam.

2 Measure the quilt width with the borders added and attach the top and bottom borders in the same way.

3 The finished butt border.

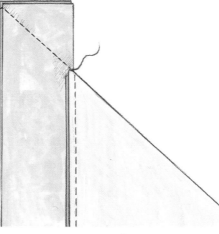

2 Turn the quilt top over to the wrong side and fold diagonally so that the top and side border edges are parallel. Using the diagonal guide on the quilter's ruler, draw a line with a soft pencil extending from the fold in the quilt top. Machine stitch from the centre out. Trim 7.5mm (¹/4in) away from the stitched line, cut and press the seam allowances open.

JOINING BACKING FABRIC

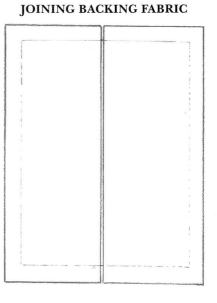

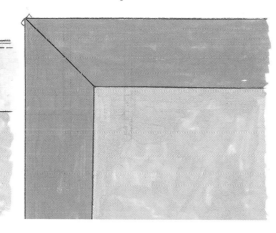

Mitred border

1 Measure the quilt top as described above, adding to the length the measurement of the width of the borders multiplied by two. Attach the two side borders as for the butt borders, starting and stopping sewing 7.5mm (¹/4in) from each end. Press. Attach the top and bottom borders, again starting and stopping a 7.5mm (¹/4in) seam allowance from the edges of the quilt. Press.

3 The finished mitred border.

It is sometimes necessary to join two pieces of backing fabric to make a piece large enough for the quilt. The direction of a join is usually decided by the most economical use of the width of fabric available, the leftover fabric being stored for future use. It is sensible not to place the backing joins immediately over major joins in the quilt top as they cause problems when quilting.

Techniques

LAYERING OR SANDWICHING

Once the top of the quilt has been completed, the next step is to layer or sandwich it together with the wadding and backing. It may be necessary to make joins in both the backing and the wadding as they should be at least 5cm (2in) larger than the quilt top on all sides.

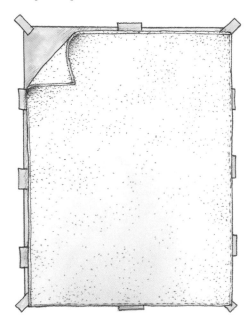

1 Place the newly pressed backing fabric right side down on a flat surface, with the grain parallel to the table edges. If you do not have a table big enough, use the floor. Using bulldog clips or masking tape, pull the fabric so that it lies taut and flat. The backing need not be as tight as a drum. Next lay the wadding in place over the backing. Gently pat flat any bumps.

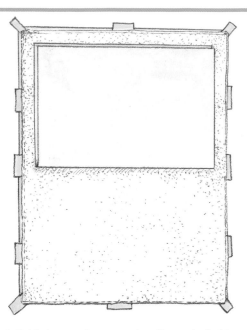

2 Fold the newly pressed quilt top in half, right sides together. Place the top, so that the fold is centred and open it up flat. Check to see that the top has an equal distance overlap on all four sides.

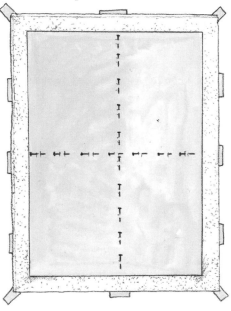

3 Start pin tacking (see page 105) across in the centre from end to end, side to side. Continue pin tacking as instructed in each project. Stitched tacking may be used.

ATTACHING BINDING

Measure and attach binding as for borders (see page 102). Insetting or setting in the binding means attaching it approximately 5cm (2in) in from the cut edge. This gives a wide binding which can be useful if either the top or the backing is narrower and the quilt would lose width by trimming. The binding is cut twice the width of the distance it is to be set in with an extra 2cm (³/4in) seam allowance added.

An alternative and simple way of binding is to bring the backing fabric round over the edge to the front and turn in a seam allowance. This also works in reverse.

Folding towards the back. Binding is normally cut 3.5–4cm (1¹/4–1¹/2in) wide. After straightening (see page 102), and working on the sides first, measure down the centre of the quilt as for the borders (see page 102). Add seam allowances and measure and cut the binding strips. Pin the binding to the edge of the quilt, right sides together, using horizontal pins. Machine stitch 7.5mm (¹/4in) from the edge of the binding. Finger press (see page 101) and join the top and bottom bindings in the same way.

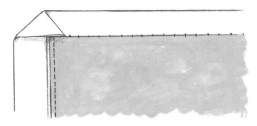

Butt corners

1 Starting on one side, fold, then pin the binding to the back of the quilt.

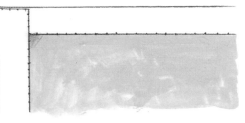

2 At the corner, make a square double fold and pin. Slip stitch along all sides and corners.

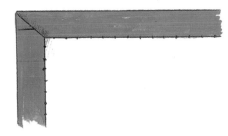

Mitred corners

1 Starting on one side, fold, then pin the binding to the back of the quilt. Fold in the diagonal corner then make a diagonal tuck on one side of the corner strip and pin.

2 Make a second diagonal fold at right angles, pin, then slip stitch.

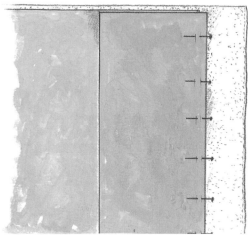

Setting in a wide binding. A wide binding is a useful way to enlarge a quilt up to 5cm (2in) on each side. It can be used by making the backing larger than the quilt, or vice versa if the backing is too small.

Measure all around the quilt and cut enough binding twice the width of the distance it is to be set in (see individual projects), plus seam allowances of 2cm (3/4in). Pin the binding horizontally, insetting it the required distance from the edge, and sew. Finger press. Measure and cut the top and bottom in the same way and sew. Fold to the back, turn in a seam allowance and slip stitch.

PIN TACKING

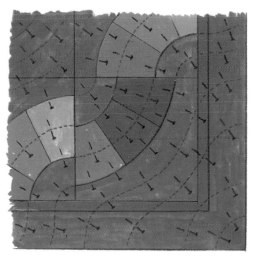

Very fine safety or special fine, long quilter's pins can be used for pin tacking. It is a matter of personal choice whether to pin horizontally across the quilting line, or straight along and pull out the pins just before the machine needle reaches the spot. Of course, horizontal pins can also be pulled out as the needle approaches.

Occasionally fingers get pricked and a spot of blood is found on the quilt top. Pull off a length of white cotton thread from a reel and chew it into a soggy ball. Using a forefinger, gently roll the ball over the blood spot, replacing it with a clean ball, if necessary. Leave to dry – magic!

MARKING QUILTING LINES

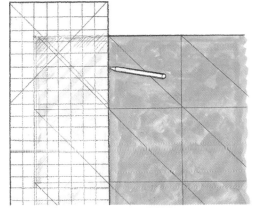

Quilting designs should be marked up on the pieced top after it has had a final press and before pinning to the wadding and backing. A light touch is needed as marks should not show on the finished quilt. A sliver of soap works well on dark fabrics. Any residual marks can be gently dabbed with a damp cloth. Special, fine lead quilter's pencils work well on light fabrics. Never use biro and test fadeaway or water-soluble pens first. Do not press after using these pens or you will never get the marks out.

Masking tape, cut to shape, can be used as quilting guides, but a residue of glue will build up on the needle if it pierces the plastic. Do not leave any sticky templates on the quilt overnight or in the sun or they will stain the fabric. It is also possible to sew through a design drawn on paper pinned to the quilt and later torn away.

MACHINE QUILTING

Before starting to machine quilt, clean out any fluff from under the feed dogs and oil the machine following the manufacturer's instructions. Lengthen the stitch slightly. Except when using nylon monofilament, fill the bobbin with the same type of thread to be used on the top. The thread need not be the same colour. Take time to understand how the tension on your machine works; it is a matter of balance. Read the instructions and practise on a spare piece of fabric from the quilt, using the identical wadding and backing. If the bottom thread shows through on the top stitching, either tighten the top tension or loosen the lower tension. Do not be afraid to experiment.

It is important to sit comfortably while you work. Set the machine to the right of the table, with room for the quilt to travel to the back of the machine. Place another table to the left and slightly behind to help support the weight. Sit opposite the needle, rather than dead centre of the machine. Tension advice has been given in the projects, where needed.

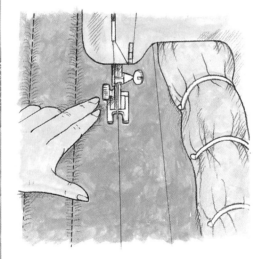

Machine quilting To allow the bulk of the quilt to pass under the sewing machine arm, roll the right hand side of the quilt into a long sausage and hold it in place with bicycle clips, or make a similar shape from wire coathangers.

Work from the centre, gradually moving across the unrolled section to the outer edge, then reverse the procedure. At the start of a line of machining, hang the quilt over your shoulder so that it does not catch under the tray. Work a few very small stitches, length 1/4, so that the thread does not unravel, then lengthen the stitch to 3 and continue sewing. Try not to push, but let the walking foot and feed dogs move the quilt along. Bumps can be eased under the foot using the forefinger and second finger placed close to the foot, moving all three layers, rather than pulling from behind.

Free-machine quilting Free machine quilting is worked with the feed dogs in the down position, or covered by a special plate, supplied with the machine if it needs it. Without the feed dogs to move the fabric after each stitch has been formed it is necessary to steer the fabric manually. Hold the fabric firmly with splayed fingers either side of the needle. The size of the stitches will depend on how fast the motor is run and how much the fabric is moved. Work out routes which will avoid too much stopping, starting and tying off ends.

Drop or cover the feed dogs. Thread the machine with the same weight thread on the top and bobbin. It may be necessary to tighten the bobbin screw. Attach a darning

foot and slide the quilt under the foot. Lower the foot lever. Make a stitch where the quilting is to start and pull the bobbin thread to the top. Hold both threads firmly and make two or three very small stitches before lengthening the stitch to around 3, or 9–12 stitches to 2.5cm (1in). Keeping the machine at a constant fast speed, move the fabric, "drawing the design" with the needle.

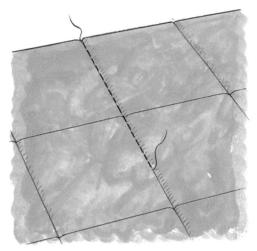

Quilting in the ditch Quilting in the ditch is a useful way to secure the quilt layers prior to free machine quilting. It is also a neat solution if stitches on the surface of the quilt are likely to interfere with the patchwork design. Using the walking foot, stitch close to the join on the opposite side to the seam allowances, pulling the fabric from the sides to open "the ditch".

FINISHING OFF To finish at the end of a line of stitching, turn the quilt to the wrong side. Grasp the end of the thread showing on the back, pull so that a loop of the front thread shows and hook it through, using the end of a pin. Tie a reef knot, right thread over left, then left thread over right. Using an embroidery needle with a long eye, pass the two threads through the eye, and sew in, near the point of exit, on the back of the quilt. Bring the needle out about 2.5cm (1in) away and cut off the thread ends. Check that the stitch has not gone through onto the front.

PIVOTING

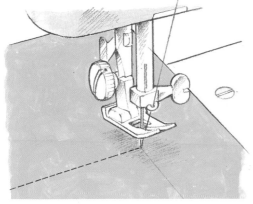

To turn a right-angle corner, leave the needle in the down position, lift the presser foot lever, rotate the work, lower the presser foot lever and continue stitching.

KNOTTING

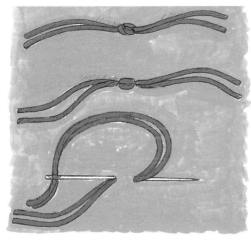

Quilt layers can be held together by knotting, which is often decorative, but is also used to secure the ends of threads. Always use a cotton thread, which will not unravel. Stranded embroidery thread works well. Thread an embroidery needle with a double length of yarn and, starting from the front of the quilt, leaving a tail, make two stitches in the same spot. Knot the right thread over the left, then the left over the right, and cut the thread, leaving tails of the desired length.

MAKING A HANGING SLEEVE

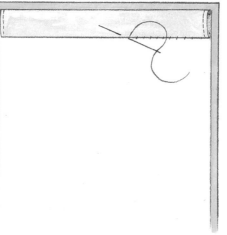

Quilts to be shown in exhibitions and, of course, wallhangings need a narrow hanging sleeve through which a flat batten can pass. Cut a strip of fabric 11cm (4¹/₄in) wide, the length should be the same as the width of the quilt. Turn in a hem at either end and press in a seam allowance along one long edge. At the point of attaching the top binding to the quilt, add the hanging sleeve to the backing side, sewing in the unpressed edge at the same time. After the binding has been sewn, slip stitch the binding and the sleeve to the back of the quilt, allowing a little ease to accommodate the batten. Take care not to let the stitches show on the right side.

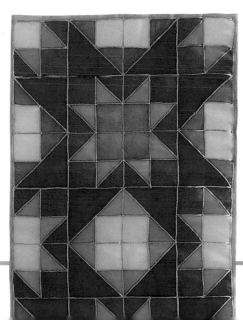

MAKING A SILK PAINTING FRAME

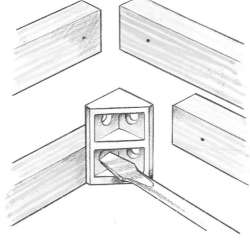

1 Cut two pieces of 20 x 9mm (³/₄ x ³/₈in) planed softwood 33cm (13in) in length, and two 66cm (26in). Rub down all the surfaces with fine sandpaper. Lay out the four pieces of wood and mark where the overlap and screw will be with the plastic corner block in place. Drill a pilot hole, and screw the first side together.

2 Hold the next piece of wood at right angles and screw the second side of the corner block in place. Repeat for the other three corners. You will see how the corner block serves as a "leg" and stops the gutta or silk from touching the worktop.

SUPPLIERS

The publisher and author should like to thank the following stockists, distributors and manufacturers for their interest and enthusiasm during the making of the quilts in this book.

COTTON

Diana Peters,
13 Stourton Road,
Ainsdale,
Merseyside PR8 3PL

John Kaldor,
Portland House,
4 Great Portland Street,
London W1N 5AA.

Liberty of London Ltd,
Regent Street,
London W1R 6AH.

**Natural Charm Solids fabric
Ebor International Fabrics,**
Embsay Mills,
Embsay,
Skipton,
North Yorkshire BD23 6QF.

Rose & Hubble,
2/4 Relay Road,
White City,
London W12 7SJ

FELT

B. Brown,
79-89 Pentonville Road,
London N1 9LW.

SILKS

James Hare Ltd,
Monarch House,
PO Box 72,
Queen Street,
Leeds LS1 1LX.

Rose & Hubble,
2/4 Relay Road,
White City,
London W12 7SJ.

THREADS

Madeira Threads (UK) Ltd,
Thirsk Industrial Park,
York Road,
Thirsk,
North Yorkshire YO7 3BX.

Coats Patons Crafts,
PO Box 22,
McMullen Road,
Darlington,
Co. Durham DL1 1YQ.

EMBROIDERY THREADS

DMC Creative World Ltd,
Pullman Road,
Wigston,
Leicestershire LE18 2DY.

FABRIC PAINTS

Dylon International Ltd,
Worsley Bridge Road,
London SE26 5HD.

Art Van Go,
16 Hollybush Lane,
Datchworth,
Herts SG3 6RE.

RIBBONS

Panda Ribbons,
Selectus Ltd,
Elm Tree Workshops,
Hitcham,
Suffolk IP7 7LJ.

TEMPLATE PLASTIC AND EQUIPMENT (MAIL ORDER)

Creative Grids,
PO Box 207,
Leicester LE3 6YP.

WADDING

Fairfield Processing Corporation,
W. Williams & Son,
Regent House,
1 Thane Villas,
London N7 7PH.

The G & G Quilt Company,
52 Swan Lane,
Coventry CV2 4GB.

METRIC & IMPERIAL GRAPHPAPER

Tollit & Harvey Ltd,
Oldmedow Road,
Hardwick Industrial Estate,
Kings Lynn,
Norfolk PE30 4LW.

TOOLS AND EQUIPMENT (MAIL ORDER)

Quilt Basics,
2 Meades Lane,
Chesham,
Bucks HP5 1ND.

EMBROIDERY SUPPLIES (MAIL ORDER)

Barnyarns Ltd,
Langrish,
Petersfield,
Hants GU32 1RQ

SEWING MACHINES

Bernina Sewing Machines,
Bogod Machine Company,
50-52 Great Sutton Street,
London EC1V 0DJ.

SPECIALIST QUILT SHOPS AND MAIL ORDER

Creative Quilting,
3 Bridge Road,
East Molesey,
Surrey KT8 9EU.
Tel. 0181 941 7075

Greenhill Patchwork & Quilting,
27 Bell Street,
Romsey,
Hampshire SO51 8GY.
Tel. 01794 517973

Maple Textiles craft shop,
188-190 Maple Road,
Penge,
London SE20 8HT.
Tel. 0181 659 8049

Patchworks and Quilts,
9 West Place,
Wimbledon,
London SW19 4UH.
Tel. 0181 946 1643

Piecemakers,
13 Manor Green Road,
Epsom,
Surrey KL19 0RA
Tel: 01372 743161

Quilters Haven,
Rendlesham Mews,
Rendlesham,
Woodbridge,
Suffolk IP12 2SZ.
Tel. 01394 461183

**Strawberry Fayre
(mail order only),**
Chagford,
Devon TQ13 8EN.
Tel. 01647 433250

The Sewing Machine Centre,
45 Crellin Street,
Barrow-in-Furness,
Cumbria LA14 1DS.
Tel. 012229 823714

ACKNOWLEDGEMENTS

Grateful thanks to Ruth Jarman for her invaluable advice and machine quilting skills on Blues in the Night, Birds in the Air, Amish Fans, Poppies, Dyeing for Bed, Animals at Bedtime, Cherubs, Strippy Quilt, Deco Delight, and for her appliqué skills on Ribbon Knot Garden, Ring-a-Roses and Art Nouveau.

Many thanks also to the following quilters for their generous help and interest. The Log Cabin and Sashiko quilts were made by Pat Taylor, the Bow Ties Quilt by June Barnes, the Star Quilt by Carolyn Forster, and Threadlines by Jan Hale. The Dyeing for Bed fabric was dyed by Leslie Morgan. Poppies was stencilled by Caroline Brown. Quality control and help with finishing the quilts was given by Shirley Bartlett, and Jenny Rayment and Lynne Edwards inspired Bow Ties.

I should also like to thank the following team for helping to make this beautiful book. Robert Claxton for his broad shoulders; Steve Tanner who enhanced the quilts with his photography, and his assistant, Mary; Pamela Westland for her generosity and flowers; Adèle Hayward for her enthusiasm and endless patience. Stonecastle Graphics for their book design skills; John Hutchinson for his clear step by step illustrations; Tim Jefferson, and the many friends who lent props.

The publishers would like to thank the following for supplying properties for photography: Avant Garden, 77 Ledbury Road, Notting Hill, London W11 2AG (page 67); A Barnful of Brass Beds, Manor Farm, St. Judith's Lane, Sawtry, Cambridgeshire PE7 5XE (page 63); Debenhams plc, Oxford Street, London W1 (pages 59 and 77); Deptich Designs, 7 College Fields, Prince Georges Road, London SW19 2PT (page 53); The Oriental Rug Company, 42 Verulam Road, St Albans, Herts, AL3 4DQ (page 53); Staks Trading Ltd, 31 Thames Street, Kingston-upon-Thames, KT1 1PH (pages 81 and 84).

CREDITS

Managing Editor: Jo Finnis

Editor: Adèle Hayward

Design: Stonecastle Graphics Ltd

Photography: Steve Tanner

Photographic Direction: Stonecastle Graphics Ltd

Illustrations: John Hutchinson

Production: Ruth Arthur; Neil Randles; Paul Randles; Karen Staff; Jonathan Tickner

Production Director: Gerald Hughes